MW00469738

TAKE YOUR LUNCH BREAK

TAKE YOUR LUNCH BREAK

HELPFUL TIPS FOR RELIEVING WORK-RELATED STRESS

MASSOMA ALAM CHOHAN

NEW DEGREE PRESS

COPYRIGHT © 2021 MASSOMA ALAM CHOHAN

TAKE YOUR LUNCH BREAK
Helpful Tips for Relieving Work-Related Stress

ISBN   978-1-63676-855-7 *Paperback*
        978-1-63730-187-6 *Kindle Ebook*
        978-1-63730-299-6 *Ebook*

In the Name of God, the Most Beneficent, the Most Merciful.

All the praises and thanks be to God.

To all those with anxiety, I see you and I hear you.

To my beloved parents, Hyder and Unsar, for always being my biggest supporters and my number one fans.

To my siblings, Monis, Mohammad, and Fathima, for always having my back.

To my husband, Omar, who accepted me in my worst days and loved me anyway.

To my children, Rayaan and Amira, this one is for you.

CONTENTS

"One day you will tell your story of how you overcame what you went through and it will be someone else's survival guide."

—BRENÉ BROWN

INTRODUCTION

"Massoma, it's unacceptable that you've been coming in to work late and leaving early," my boss said and lowered her horn-rimmed glasses to slightly above her nostrils, her eyes peering over. In her perfect pencil skirts and no-nonsense attitude, she reminded me of Meryl Streep in *The Devil Wears Prada.*

I gulped. This was my annual performance evaluation for a nonprofit startup where I had wanted to work and make a difference in the world, but instead I felt deflated. I was afraid to speak, fearful that a tremble in my voice would uncover my trepidation, "I-I do all my—"

"Optics are key. Your coworkers are complaining you're not here when *they* are." She crossed her arms and looked at me expectantly.

It's true I would come to work late and leave early—not because I was lazy, but because I wanted to escape the workplace environment (I would make up or do more work at home). A few times, I broke down at work and started crying. I was lucky to have some supportive coworkers who were there to console me. I felt so embarrassed and annoyed that I had let myself cry at work, but I really couldn't help it.

There was no way I could possibly discuss this with my boss. I admired her authority and presence so much, and she seemed like everything I wasn't. People listened to her when she spoke. In contrast, I was timid and soft-spoken. I wanted to be more like her and not be pushed around by my emotions. I would get peeved by my feelings. I was almost afraid of her, and I felt it was impossible to show her my vulnerability.

She also told me some of my work wasn't up to the standards she had. I felt like crying after the meeting, but I held it in until I got home, where I collapsed to the floor in tears. My performance evaluation gave me even more anxiety than I already felt. As a straight-A student, my poor work performance did not align with my self-image. I wanted to be the best, but I was falling short.

My anxiety followed me everywhere, including the workplace, and affected my productivity, attention span, and work quality. I felt anxious on my twenty-five-minute commute on the highway to work, then getting on the elevator and going up to a higher floor awakened my fear of heights. My heart would race as I would try to meet deadlines, and the amount of work I had to complete was overwhelming. I would eat lunch at my desk while working—almost everybody did; it was the job culture there. I hardly took any breaks or left my desk. My work station was messy, strewn with papers and files. You could see from my desk I was disorganized, and my mind was frantic.

Before I spoke in meetings, my hands would get cold and clammy, and my legs would shake. I would get hot and sweaty, and my mouth would become dry. I never thought it was possible to feel cold and hot simultaneously, but here I was. I would always worry about whether my work was good enough, if I was good enough, if I said the right words, if I sounded smart or stupid. My worries greatly impacted my performance. My anxiety hindered my growth, and my stress over my productivity made me perform poorly.

I knew I needed to make changes. I worked incredibly hard on my anxiety. This wasn't how I wanted to live my life or how I wanted to spend my time at work. Desperately searching for some kind of "cure" for my anxiety, I started reading countless self-help books. I went to a therapist weekly. I tried cognitive behavioral therapy as well as other therapies while taking anti-anxiety medications.

All of these resources helped my anxiety, and I did start to feel better, but my anxiety was still there, lingering over me like a black cloud. I would obsessively think about how difficult my life was, and my anxiety was becoming a core part of my identity. My mind was always racing. I believed I would always have this crippling anxiety. Despite all my efforts to try to find some solution, nothing helped.

After nine years of being in therapy, being on medications, and reading many books, something finally clicked.

I finally overcame my anxiety.

THE ROOTS OF MY ANXIETY

An essential part of overcoming my anxiety was understanding where it stemmed from.

"Your daughter has a slim chance of survival," the doctors told my parents. I was fifteen years old, hospitalized for a systemic illness called acute respiratory distress syndrome (ARDS). Both of my lungs were filled with fluid, and I couldn't breathe without a ventilator. A central venous catheter inserted into my neck delivered drugs straight into my bloodstream, and you can still see the scars on my neck from the line. The doctors placed me in a medically-induced coma. Despite these efforts, my prognosis was grim, and the doctors told my parents and family there was little chance I would wake up.

Let's backtrack a little. Right before my hospitalization, my family and I had gone to Philadelphia for vacation. We rode on a beautiful horse-drawn carriage, looking at the Old City and colonial buildings. When we returned home to Buffalo, New York, we expected everything to go back to normal. A few days later, my temperature spiked to 104°F.

I was hospitalized and then rushed in an ambulance to the nearest children's hospital, which was about an hour away. That feeling of fear and uncertainty—the experience of struggling with every breath—was excruciating, and I would not wish it upon my worst enemy. As the siren screamed, it pulled the breath from my lungs; my breathing was even more labored. An intense feeling of anxiety was now blinding me. I had never experienced anxiety like this before.

Once I arrived at the children's hospital, I screamed uncontrollably for my parents and my doctors to help me. They wheeled me away into the ICU. That was the last thing I remembered, then, darkness.

I woke up two weeks later. When I looked in the mirror, I didn't even recognize myself. "How long has it been?" I asked my mother, sitting by my bedside with tired eyes and prayer beads in her hand. "Too long, my dear daughter," she replied in Punjabi as she broke down in tears.

After two weeks in the ICU, I fought my way to a second chance at life. I woke up and could breathe by myself again. After another week in recovery, I was discharged. I was ecstatic to be leaving the hospital and going home. I had lost over twenty pounds, and most of the muscles in my legs had atrophied. Walking up and down stairs was difficult. Life wouldn't be the same for a while, but to many, I looked normal.

Many people, including physicians, tend to ignore the mental consequences of hospitalization. The end of my hospitalization was only the beginning of my anxiety and panic disorder. This traumatic experience took a huge emotional toll on me. I would often cry, especially at night, recollecting my memories of the hospitalization. At the time, I did not fully process what I had been through. Unprocessed traumatic experiences can cause anxiety. Even hearing a beeping sound would cause me to start feeling anxious, as it reminded me of the hospital life support machines.

It took me years to process what had happened. I would experience moments of depersonalization, which is the feeling that you are observing yourself from outside your body and the sense life around you is not real. I would call it "weird feelings" because I had no idea what was happening. I kept it to myself for years and just pushed through. Nobody even knew. I thought I was going crazy, but it was easier to ignore these sensations than to face them.

I didn't get officially diagnosed with an anxiety disorder until I was twenty-two years old. At that time, I was finishing up my first semester of medical school. The stress and pressure of medical school was a huge trigger, and my anxiety flared up. No one ever forgets their first panic attack. I was walking to my class when, unexpectedly, my heart rate increased. I felt out of place, confused, dizzy. I got hot, and my palms started to sweat; my muscles tensed up. It was one of the most frightening experiences I have had, and I had no idea what was happening to me.

Two years after my first panic attack, my anxiety became crippling. I became agoraphobic for about a month. I did not leave my house because I was terrified I would experience another panic attack. Halfway through medical school, I had to drop out because the anxiety consumed me. It was too mentally taxing. I could not sleep, I wasn't eating well, and I had lost weight. I was living in a constant state of fear. Can you imagine continually being afraid? That was my life. I had moments when I didn't want to live anymore; the pain was that intense.

TAKING CONTROL OF MY LIFE

After working through my anxiety and making lifestyle changes, my work performance also changed drastically. Everyone noticed, especially my boss. I was more productive and less stressed. I was meeting my deadlines and wasn't dreading going to work. I had better interpersonal relationships, and I was happier at work. I was confident in my work and meetings, and it showed. My coworkers said, "Wow! You seem like a new person!" Sure, it didn't happen overnight, but I turned my stress into a vehicle for success.

Looking back, I was angry about how anxiety stole freedom from me. Anxiety controlled me. It pushed me to quit medical school, a dream I'd had since I was a child. My world became so small I was confined to my own house. I let anxiety control my life far too many years. I let anxiety become a limiting belief. I would often say to myself, "I can't do that because I have anxiety." However, my anxiety also empowered me to learn and find my inner strengths.

I believe everything happens for a reason, and I am glad it all worked out the way it did. Without my adversities,

I wouldn't be where I am today or the person I am today, so I am thankful for them. I genuinely think our difficulties can be our biggest blessings and lead us to a better life. My pain turned into purpose. Those struggles are now my strengths, and now I am in a position to help others.

I was inspired to write this book after giving a TEDx Talk on overcoming anxiety and speaking about the primary resources and approaches that helped me tackle my anxiety. I was taken aback by the overwhelming positive response I received following my talk. Afterward, I realized I still had so much more to say and many other resources to share about my journey. Having also completed my master's in industrial and organizational psychology, I wanted to apply my knowledge of psychological principles and research methods to improve the work environment.

Three months after starting this book, I became pregnant with my first child. While I was pregnant with him, I finished my first manuscript draft. I was supposed to publish the same month he was born, but caring for my newborn took priority, so I put my writing on pause. I grew comfortable becoming a mother and I continued to work on this book because I truly believe in it. Then came the COVID-19 pandemic and my second child; these changes forced me to give myself grace and persevere. The pandemic gave me more reason to continue and expand my work. We can find inner strength when we have no other choice but to rise up.

WHAT TO EXPECT FROM THIS BOOK

On my healing journey, I found dozens and dozens of different strategies for working with stress. Some of these strategies worked, and others didn't. This book has done some of this research for you, compiling and synthesizing numerous stress and anxiety-reducing strategies. I compiled many resources from years of research, personal experiences, and interviews with leaders and experts in the field. This book takes a universal approach into ways to ease stress and anxiety. While not every strategy will work for everyone, hopefully you will find various systemic approaches that will resonate with you and bring you joy so you can grow, prosper, and fulfill your purpose.

My research prompted me to go a step further and speak with professionals to find out how they experience and manage work stress. I went on LinkedIn to find people in specific fields and reached out to former colleagues and mentors who I felt would have significant stories and add value to this book. The interviews took place over four years, both in-person and virtually and include shifts the COVID-19 pandemic ushered into the workplace and our lives. Not all the interviews are in this book, but they all contributed to my understanding of how we can best manage stress and anxiety while we work. When I refer to work in this book, it will encompass working remotely as well, not just physically in the office.

You can learn to relieve, manage, or even overcome anxiety just as I have, along with many professionals I interviewed. This book shows you how in twelve value-packed chapters that explore:

- Impacts of work stress and anxiety during the pandemic and how some of these changes are good news for professionals
- The science of stress and anxiety so you can understand *why* you are feeling the way you are
- Holistic stress management so you can make small daily changes to feel and work better
- The role of therapy and the benefits of working with a mental health professional—even if you're proud
- Resilience and micro-resilience you can cultivate in yourself to be unshakable no matter what happens
- Minimalism and the benefits of decluttering your workspace—both physical and digital—to only keep what brings you peace
- How to leave stress at the door and separate your personal/work life even when you're working from home
- Strategies to navigate performance anxiety, deadlines, and procrastination so you can kick these common work stressors to the curb
- Problematic coworkers and bosses: what you need to know to be your best self
- Causes of and preventions for burnout so you can stop giving too much and exit gracefully when that's the best outcome for you
- Mindset strategies that elevate your thoughts and expectations to lower stress and anxiety
- Stress management habits from the morning, throughout the workday, and in the evening to feel in control 24/7

These teachings have helped many people conquer their anxiety and live a prosperous, happier, more productive life, and I hope the same proves true for you. I had a generalized anxiety disorder (GAD) and panic disorder (PD) for nine years and I was on medication for eight of those years. I'm happy to say I am no longer diagnosed with GAD and PD. If I can do it, so can you.

There is a way out of the feeling of dread anxiety can give you. Sure, you may still feel some anxiety here and there, but your reaction to it will not be as severe. Instead of experiencing a panic attack, you will be able to brush off moments of anxiety and move on with your life.

I hold a bachelor's in biology and psychology and a master's in industrial and organizational psychology, which is the study of human behavior in the workplace, but I am not a mental health professional. Therefore, I have not focused on using medication to address anxiety or stress symptoms. This doesn't mean I think medication isn't a good option for some people. Some of the people I talked to found anxiety medication to be extremely helpful. If you think medication might help your stress or anxiety, you should speak with your physician or with a psychiatrist. It is always a better idea to speak with a mental health professional before embarking on your stress-reduction journey.

My hopes are that this book will help many people conquer their fears and thrive at work and in their lives. This is a book for people at work, whether you are in the workplace or working from home, but many of the techniques taught in this book can be applicable to anyone, anytime.

It's time you stop allowing stress and anxiety to get in the way of living your best life. We are all here for a short time, so make it worthwhile. I truly believe God gave me a second chance at life, and I feel there is some purpose I need to fulfill. Maybe one of my purposes was to write this book, so one day you would pick it up and it would help you change your life.

Now, let's get to work!

CHAPTER ONE

THE FUTURE OF WORK

THE YEAR 2020: COVID-19

"I am positive for COVID-19."

My heart dropped as I read the text message from my brother, Mohammad, in April 2020. The pandemic had just started, and we were all in lockdown and knew next to nothing about the virus. My brother was bravely working as an internal medicine resident in a COVID-19 unit and most likely contracted it from his patients. So many questions ran through my mind as I read the text again: Is my brother going to be okay? Is he going to get more sick and have to be intubated? Who will take care of him?

He was alone, and no one could go and attend to him. It was terrifying for the rest of our family, and we felt completely helpless, especially as he was very sick for about eight days. He had extreme body aches, fever, weird dreams, and couldn't sleep well. What was amazing was seeing how many of his friends left food and medicine outside his door. Thank God he finally recovered and went right back to work in the COVID-19 units as the numbers of patients skyrocketed. In no way was this situation unique.

The year 2020 was difficult, emotional, confusing, and lonely for many people. It was filled with loss, not only of jobs, but the greater, deeper loss of loved ones. People also felt a deprivation of community as the stressful year seemed to drag on endlessly. We have all been struggling with isolation and social distancing. The closure of educational institutes, workplaces, and entertainment venues so people stay in their homes to help break the chain of transmission, while necessary, has taken a toll.

Moreover, we experienced changes in our workplace environments, both positive and negative, along with much uncertainty in the labor market. Of course, these factors can and did affect our mental health. According to an issue brief by the Kaiser Family Foundation, over half of Americans have reported mental health problems due to the pandemic and its side effects—isolation, job loss, and general stress related to the pandemic (Panchal, 2020). The work and home balance, already tenuous for many, has blurred even further. This constant state of being "on" is causing burnout to become more frequent and more real. Frontline healthcare workers are experiencing burnout. Parents are stressed about their children's mental and social development, and there is a current shortage of mental health treatment professionals (Panchal, 2020). All in all, the pandemic has posed a serious threat to the mental wellbeing of almost every discernible demographic group.

We face a collective problem with the pandemic, and it has also served as an invitation for us to use our isolation as a moment to look inward and decide what we really want and what we are willing to tolerate in our work or in the workplace. In this chapter, I briefly establish what I mean by "stress" and "anxiety," before diving into some ways these factors are impacting the changing landscape of work, as well as the inner selves of our workforce.

SHIFTING STRESS

Stress is your body's reaction to a specific trigger, or a response to a stimulus, and it is generally a short-term experience as well as an unavoidable part of life. Interestingly, stress can be positive or negative. "Eustress" is the psychological term for good or positive stress, like challenging work (Scott, 2020). Eustress is the type of stress we feel when we are excited when we encounter a challenge. As Elizabeth Scott, a wellness coach and author, writes in an article for *VeryWell*, "Not striving for goals, not overcoming challenges, not having a reason to wake up in the morning would be damaging to us, so eustress is considered 'good' stress. It keeps us healthy and happy." Stress isn't always an enemy.

Some of us don't perceive all sources of stress as a "challenge." Sometimes, stressors feel like threats, and then it's considered negative stress. Research shows, "when an event is perceived as a 'threat,' we respond to it differently than if it's seen as a 'challenge.' Threats tend to elicit a greater stress response from us and create greater levels of anxiety" (Scott, 2020). Threats can be intimidating, and certainly many of us felt the threat of layoffs, business closures, and more during the pandemic. In contrast, challenges are opportunities to prove ourselves and learn how much we're capable of accomplishing when we try. If we understand this distinction, as Scott writes:

"We can view many of the stressors in our lives as challenges rather than threats merely by changing how we talk to ourselves about the challenges and by focusing on the resources we have to handle these challenges rather than focusing on what may go wrong and how damaging that would be."

When stress results in disturbances to your health, such as poor sleep, poor concentration, attention-related problems, and the inability to do the things you usually do, then it's time to take action to improve your health.

Negative job stress can also inhibit our productivity. It is important, however, to remember you should not maintain consistent expectations for yourself. The world has changed, and the amount of work you will be able to complete has also changed. The word "productive" became something of a trigger word for many this year. People struggled to get much done, and that's okay. It is okay if you were not productive in 2020 given the difficult circumstances. It's completely okay to not always be productive.

Katherine May suggests in her book *Wintering* that we all have moments of "wintering" where we need to retreat from the world, rest, and recover. At the end of the workday, I would look at what I completed, and if I was not as productive as I wanted to be, I would go into a cycle of self-loathing and guilt. "I am not smart, I am not good enough, I can't do anything right, I couldn't even complete all my tasks today!" The list goes on. The guilt we feel when we are not as productive as we would like can be harmful. Firstly, you need to take care of yourself, which is far more important than being "productive."

Stress is primarily subjective and contextual. What causes me stress may not cause you stress. For example, moving from in-person meetings to Zoom meetings might not create any stress for one employee, but can for another. Someone may feel completely confident with public speaking, while another person may feel extreme stress about speaking in public. In fact, that same person who is confident in public speaking may have previously felt stress toward speaking in front of his friends. Stress is a *reaction* to a situation; it may not be about the *actual* situation. We generally feel stressed when we believe we can't handle the demands of a problem ("OSH Answers Fact Sheets: Workplace Stress—General," 2018). If you pay attention to your thoughts, you may find yourself saying something like, "I just can't handle it. I can't do it." In actuality, more times than not we are fully capable of handling it.

If we take a deep look into our mindset about stress and view it as a driving force to better ourselves, we will be able to change our relationship with stress and say, "Yes, I'm feeling stressed right now because it's uncertain if my new boss will like me, but that's good because it will help me prepare to make a good first impression." This is what

I tell myself all the time. If you don't recognize something as a threat, there is usually no threat-based stress response. Ironically, a threat-based stress response and eustress response is similar. What differentiates them is how you interpret the physiological response you are experiencing. It's the clammy palms, sweaty foreheads, the heart palpitations, and of course that infamous sense of impending doom.

When you stop perceiving experiences as threats and see them as a challenge instead, the fear you would normally experience will turn into excitement. A wonderful, curated rush and thrill will overcome you, allowing you to make the shift in your perception by focusing on the resources you have. You'll start seeing the benefits of every situation, especially as changes in the workplace are giving way to creative solutions, we already know how to help reduce stress. I give many examples in the coming chapters when you can shift stressful moments and use a whole host of tools to do so.

ANXIETY
You may often hear people say, "Oh my goodness, I had the worst panic attack last night when I realized I had to submit a proposal to my boss today!" or, "I feel so anxious about the upcoming meeting where I have to present my proposition!" The words "panic attack" and "anxiety" are commonly used by those who don't have anxiety disorders. However, there is a distinction between anxiety and anxiety disorder. The "anxiety" we know colloquially as a persistent mental health disorder that can be induced by

stress is called generalized anxiety disorder (GAD) by the scientific community. To be diagnosed with GAD, you'll need to see a psychologist or psychiatrist.

In writing this book, I interviewed psychologist Dr. Erin Grinstead. She shared this definition of anxiety: "Anxiety is a feeling that originates internally in response to stress. It's a feeling of persistent dread or apprehension." The basis of cognitive behavioral therapy (CBT), a common treatment for anxiety, is the idea anxiety is often caused by what we tell ourselves in a situation, the internal dialogue. Anxiety can persist after the stressor is over because it's an internal response.

People who suffer from anxiety disorders might worry excessively about a future danger and have an unreasonable amount of fear of a perceived threat, which can include a specific phobia, such as a fear of flying, animals, or elevators. There are many types and subtypes of anxiety and diagnostic criteria for each disorder. If you think your "stress" may qualify as an "anxiety" diagnosis, see a mental health care professional because there are many who have GAD but have not been officially diagnosed. The Anxiety and Depression Association of America estimates more than 18 percent of the population has an anxiety disorder. Yet only 36 percent of those with the disorder get help. Globally, about 1 in 13 people suffer from anxiety ("Facts and Statistics," 2021).

Although you may have noticed stress and anxiety are closely linked, they aren't the same. Here's one key way in which they differ: Stress alleviates after the situation passes, like giving a speech. However, anxiety doesn't just go away after the perceived threat has been eliminated. It's chronic and can happen when there isn't a known trigger. Anxiety can also cause the same disturbances to your health as negative stress. Similar to stress, anxiety disorders can affect employees' performance at work, their work quality, their relationships with colleagues, and their relationships with supervisors. I know it sounds confusing since they are so alike. Think of stress as something normal everybody experiences and an anxiety disorder as a more severe, amplified form of stress that can become debilitating.

For some people with an anxiety disorder, the discomfort caused by anxiety is far from normal and can be wholly debilitating. Anxiety disorders can affect every aspect of a person's life: their personal relationships, physical health, and performance in the workplace. With regards to performance at work, anxiety can impact quality of the work, relationships with colleagues, and relationships with supervisors. In the coming chapters, I share many strategies for navigating these issues and ways the changing workplace is opening new possibilities to accommodate those with anxiety.

On a final note, panic attacks and anxiety attacks are closely linked, but the intensity is greater in a panic attack. Panic attacks are sudden, intense feelings of fear of disaster or losing control that usually peak within a few minutes and can happen even when there's no apparent threat. For example, I was sitting at my desk working away when all of a sudden, I felt a rush of heat flow through my body. I felt like I was about to lose control and I couldn't catch my breath, like an elephant was sitting on my chest.

Panic attacks can happen anytime, and many people who experience panic attacks feel a sense of dread because they don't know when the next panic attack will come. You can have a panic attack without having an anxiety disorder diagnosis (Kamphaus, 2013). These days when more of us are working from home and we understand anxiety better than ever before, we have more options, which I discuss in the coming chapters.

CHALLENGES IN THE WORKPLACE

In response to the current COVID-19 situation, the workplace is changing rapidly and so are our stress and anxiety. As William Arruda explains in his *Forbes* article, "6 Ways COVID-19 Will Change the Workplace Forever," some of these changes—such as increased corporate flexibility, the possibility of working from home, and an emphasis on the social qualities of the workplace—actually have the potential to improve some workplace stressors. These changes have also introduced new factors that can cause workplace stress.

According to one survey Matthew Gavidia cites in *The American Journal of Managed Care*, nearly seven in ten employees said the pandemic has been the most stressful part of their career. Parents did not only have to work from home while taking care of their children; they were also expected to be their children's teacher. This added a different layer of stress that was never before experienced. Remote employees never get to really "leave work" because their home is now their office, and their laptop/email is always on. This adds another dynamic of workplace stress. There is definite change happening, with workplaces evolving and COVID-19 affecting workplace stress.

NYU professor Steve Galloway examines the changes wrought by the pandemic in *Post Corona: From Crisis to Opportunity*. He suggested these changes are in fact just sped-up versions of patterns that had been set in motion already. The power of technology companies could already be seen pre-pandemic, and this has only increased, for example. Social changes had been exposing how industries like higher education were out-of-date, and the pandemic has made that even clearer. All these changes are creating new and different stressors, but it's also possible we can see these shifts as "challenges" and find positive stress in them.

In fact, people in the workplace must find the challenge in these changes and lean into it. In an interview with Amador, Christina Disler shares, "If you ask me, the new normal is moment by moment. We can do our best to plan and think about the future, but what we should really take out of this whole experience (the pandemic and not knowing what will happen in the next week, let alone the next month or year) is we need to do a better job as individuals and organizations to develop our resilience" (Amador, 2020). Much of this book is devoted to ways we can take care of ourselves and our mental health in the face of changing or stressful and uncertain work conditions.

Employees are also more stressed than ever about health and finances, both areas severely tested by the pandemic, with women affected the most. Corporate America faces a new emergency: many women actively consider leaving the workforce or deprioritizing their careers. Megan Cassella reports in *Politico*, "Taking into account how the labor force was growing pre-pandemic, 2.3 million fewer women are working now than would have been without the disruption." Job loss has not only disproportionately affected women, but also particularly women of color. Thomas Franck and Nate Rattner of *CNBC* report in March of 2021, "total employment for Black women is 9.7% lower than it was in February 2020, before COVID-19 hit the US, with that figure for Hispanic women close behind at 8.6% lower." In contrast, the figures for white men and women were 5 percent and 5.4 percent (Franck, 2021). This reality is a terrible blow for the hard-earned and painfully slow progress for gender diversity and equality, with companies losing women leaders, present or future.

The grim reality behind these changes are those of entrenched gender roles: during the pandemic, mothers were taking on most of the house and childcare responsibilities—three times more than fathers. That equates to being 1.5 times more likely to be covering those responsibilities for at least three hours more every day. Working mothers had already faced heightened levels of stress with working the double shift outside work and housework. The pandemic has taken away the little support available to such working women, like in-person school and childcare, making the tenuous situation worse.

Some companies are taking notice of these challenges and working with women and all their employees to create more balance in the workplace. Goals are reset with smaller scopes, or with extensions for the same goals, allowing people time to process their emotions and what's happening in our new reality. Some companies have gotten creative in this endeavor, for example, giving parents "COVID-19 days" to prepare for the upcoming school year. Others have decided to give employees several extended weekends by including Fridays every quarter.

CHANGES IN WORK-LIFE BALANCE

I am personally a very social person. I enjoy going to work physically and seeing my coworkers. I value the relationships I have with people and prefer in-person connection. There's just something about grabbing a cup of tea or coffee on your way to work and making another fresh batch once you arrive while you mingle with your coworkers about the exciting and mundane events happening in your life. The initial COVID-19 lockdown was quite difficult for me because I couldn't see my friends and be as social as I normally am. Video calls just don't quite have the same appeal as face-to-face time for me.

However, now with workplaces opening back up, more people are preferring remote work. Many people love working from home mainly because of the flexibility, myself included. Now that I have two kids, remote work is more appealing to me because of the convenience and how it positively shifted my work-life balance, and I'm not alone. In "Why Working from Home Will Stick," Stanford researchers Jose Maria Barrero, Nicholas Bloom, and Steven J. Davis share the outcomes of their survey of seventeen thousand American workers to explore how, why, and whether the changes in the workplace will continue. The outcomes are overwhelming, with 23.9 percent of the respondents saying they would "rarely" or "never" want to work from home going forward. Almost as strong, 27.3 percent indicated working from home five days a week would suit them best. The other 48.9 percent would be happy to work from home between one and four days a week. When given the choice, we want to get off the hamster wheel of commuting to a nine-to-five job and have a better balance between work and life.

The workplace challenges I outline in the previous section of this chapter offer a chance to define a work-life balance in ways that decrease stress and anxiety. This can be accomplished by adopting new set expectations for the workplace. Some examples would be meetings having clearly defined hour limits, a policy for email response outside of work hours, and clarified communication about availability. Not only would these ideas decrease daily stressors, but they also provide meaningful respite to those experiencing anxiety and anxiety disorders.

Flexibility in work hours should be made available and taken a step further to ensure employees are taking advantage of those options. Because of attached stigma, there might be reluctance in utilizing this, so leaders should address this flexibility clearly and in practice. One way this can be achieved is by evaluating performance through results and not hours. Leaders who can exemplify this shift in metrics would be the best line of action toward encouraging employees to engage in flexible options, as actions do speak louder than words. Combined efforts from company leadership and team members can help prevent employees from quitting or downshifting careers because of stress.

Moreover, while performance reviews are an integral aspect of employee evaluation, the circumstances have changed by remote work schedules and additional stress surrounding the pandemic on different fronts. The pre-COVID-19 evaluation parameters may be outdated and as such should be reexamined and tailored to fit current employee needs and situations. In setting more attainable goals, employers can do their part in preventing employee burnout, which will be beneficial to the company in the long run.

We're already seeing some good news on this front. Mental health services are now an essential part of almost all organizations. Many employees lack knowledge of this, however, as well as awareness of helpful programs, including parenting resources and bereavement counseling. Making these services well-known across the company would be beneficial for both employees and companies.

While you're advocating for these changes in your workplace, there are many things shared in this book that you can do to improve and find help for your mental health in the meantime. If the workplace has an employee assistance program, contacting them can help in getting direct counseling or referrals to mental health professionals. Aside from the workplace, primary care providers can assist in this process as well; finding and contacting mental health professionals directly is another option. There are also organizations specifically created for helping in situations like this. The National Alliance on Mental Illness (NAMI) and the Substance Abuse and Mental Health Services Administration (SAMHSA) are two such resources.

CONCLUSION

The COVID-19 pandemic has served to accelerate changes in the workplace and exacerbate existing issues to the point at which they're finally being seriously addressed. With a good understanding of what stress is and how it operates in ways that can be either positive or negative, we can find ways to navigate through it. It's important to understand how stress and anxiety can be related, but aren't the same thing, as they are often conflated in our culture. However, many solutions for workplace stress reduction can also alleviate some pressure from those diagnosed with anxiety disorders. We're already seeing changes in the workplace to take mental health more seriously, and there are many things we can do as individuals in the meantime to improve our mental health. In the next chapter, I explore stories of stress and anxiety in the workplace and the benefits of understanding what's going on inside of us so we can better deal with the day to day.

CHAPTER TWO

DIVING INTO THE SCIENCE OF ANXIETY AND STRESS

Her hands were trembling, her legs shaking, and her heart racing. She had no idea why she was feeling this way. Anxiety would appear unannounced and consume her, disrupting both her professional and personal life. Anxiety had debilitated Robyn Short, founder and president of Workplace Peace Institute, a consulting and research firm that brings peace and dignity to the workplace. When I interviewed her, she recounted how she had experienced these physical sensations for as long as she could remember. She would frequently think, "What is wrong with me? When will this end?"

I'm sure some of you will relate to her struggles, because I sure did. Like Short, you might have sought help from a medical professional. Short was diagnosed with generalized anxiety disorder (GAD), but an accurate diagnosis is only the beginning of confronting anxiety disorders. She pursued different modalities of treatment from cognitive behavioral therapy to pharmacological. At one point, she took medication that did relieve her symptoms but also left her feeling like she "didn't care about anything." Next, her psychologist encouraged Short to turn to journaling her thoughts, actions, and emotions to understand the root of her anxiety. She spent three weeks descriptively annotating in a notebook the highs and lows of what she was experiencing. This included everything she ate, she did, and especially everything she felt. By the end of the charting process, the cause of her anxiety had revealed itself.

Short approached her psychologist with details of all her actions for the past three weeks. Together, they compared all the notes of what happened during the times of her highs and lows. They found when she experienced increased anxiety, there was a common denominator: eggs. Yes, *eggs*. By tracking her meals, the psychologist saw shortly after Short (no pun intended) had her morning meal of eggs, she would experience signs and symptoms of an anxiety. The days where she opted for an alternative source of protein, her mood was more stable. Her psychologist wasn't all too surprised as he had a level of familiarity with food causing or exacerbating changes in his patients' mood, which is why he wanted her to include what she ate in her notes.

As Short found, the body is an integrated system, and even our food choices can throw us off our game. More importantly, Short's story demonstrated a key point I want to communicate in this chapter: anxiety and stress can be triggered by preventable measures. Just like Short needed to understand the cause of her anxiety before managing it, you should aim to understand your stress and anxiety for possible root causes. This chapter describes how stress and anxiety work from a scientific perspective to help you reach this understanding. Again, I am not a mental health professional or a scientific expert. The information below is based on my research and personal experiences. The more you know about the root causes, the more easily you can ask for help to mitigate those factors in your professional life. In some cases, you can start making small changes like packing a different breakfast.

ANXIETY AND WORKPLACE STRESS

Simply put, workplace stress is stress caused by work-related stressors such as tasks, workplace relationships, work performance, and pressure. If we perceive situations and circumstances as threats rather than challenges, then workplace stress might appear, as I mentioned in Chapter One. In my interview with Dr. Grinstead, whom we met in the last chapter, she explains how you can be stressed at work without the issue being anxiety while for some it could turn into an anxiety disorder. Anxiety can be brought into the workplace. You can have anxiety that manifests at work.

Here's an example of how stress can become anxiety. Maybe you have a deadline at work that causes you stress, so there's an external stimuli that creates stress, and you begin to have anxiety-related thoughts about the deadline—catastrophic thinking such as, "I will never make this deadline and even if I do, it will be judged poorly, and I will lose my job." Then the stress can compound into an anxiety disorder if that thinking persists and spills over into other situations. So, you might carry that negative self-talk to the next project and think generally, "I'm going to fail at whatever I do. Even if I help my kids with this project at home, it won't be good enough."

If the above example is in any way familiar and you struggle with work-related stress, you're not alone. *The Globe Newswire* ran a story, "Workplace Stress on the Rise With 83 percent of Americans Frazzled by Something at Work," about a 2013 telephone survey about stress conducted by the Harris Initiative on behalf of the Everest College. The study incorporated 1,019 employed adults over age eighteen who resided within the US and were employed. The results were weighted for age, sex, geographic region, and race to align them with actual proportions in the population. The findings are quite eye-opening. Approximately 83 percent of Americans are stressed by at least one thing at work. Within that survey they found stressors included being under paid, having an unreasonable workload, having poor work-life balance, the lack of opportunity for advancement, and fear of being fired. These are just a few of the stressors further increased during the pandemic.

Victor Lipman writes in his 2020 *Forbes* article "Workplace Trend: Stress Is On The Rise" work stress is not only quite real, but it can harm employees' health and personal relationships, reaching beyond the workplace. He also finds the problem of workplace stress has been steadily getting worse for at least three decades. It has never been more important for employees and employers to understand the root causes of their stress, and to do so, let's dive into the science of stress and anxiety. Understanding this science can help us understand how to resolve or manage problems caused by negative stress and anxiety.

BRAIN AND GUT: THE SCIENCE OF STRESS AND ANXIETY

When Short felt the symptoms of anxiety in the story that opens this chapter, those sensations happened because of what was going on in her brain's chemistry. Northwestern Medicine has an infographic on their website that provides a clear description of what's going on internally when anxiety strikes: Symptoms of anxiety disorders are thought to disrupt the brain's emotional processing center rather than the higher cognitive centers. The brain's limbic system, comprising the hippocampus, amygdala, hypothalamus, and thalamus, is responsible for most of the emotional processing. Individuals with an anxiety disorder may have heightened activity in these areas.

The limbic system protected our caveman ancestors by responding to sources of danger, like bears. While terror and adrenaline can be useful if a bear is chasing you, these days we rarely get chased by bears. Although our environment has changed, our anxiety responses have remained the same. People with anxiety disorders experience the stress associated with a bear attack (or a similar danger) in inappropriate moments. So, no, it's not just in your head. You can physically feel the sensations of anxiety.

The amygdala, a part of the limbic system, handles emotionally important external stimuli and starts the appropriate behavioral reaction. The emotional response has a clear evolutionary advantage. Blogger Mark Dingman of *Neuroscientifically Challenged* provides in "Know Your Brain: Amygdala" an excellent example of how this process unfolds in an ideal situation:

"If you are walking through the grass and a snake darts out at you, you don't want to have to spend a lot of time cognitively assessing the danger the snake might pose. Instead, you want your body to experience immediate fear and jump backward without consciously initiating this action. The direct pathway from the thalamus to the amygdala may be one way to achieve this type of response."

The amygdala is in charge of the presentation of fear, aggression, and species-specific defensive behavior. The amygdala also creates and retrieves emotional and fear-related memories. It can be useful to understand that anxiety disorders can originate from a physical location in the brain. These disorders are not imaginary, and they're not your fault. They're a physical condition.

Anxiety disorders aren't just caused by some regions of the brain, though. Elizabeth I. Martin, in a September 2009 research article for *Psychiatric Clinics of North America*, notes anxiety disorders can also be caused by neurotransmitters, which connect different regions of the brain. She recounts several studies which found overactive neurotransmitters (chemicals that allow your nerves to communicate with one another) may contribute to anxiety disorders.

However, the physical signs of anxiety and stress aren't limited to our brains. When people mention they have a "gut feeling" and just know about something, they may not be wrong; our gut *does* tell us information. Medicine is starting to understand the brain-gut axis and the connection between digestion, mood, health, and thoughts. The *New England Journal of Medicine* ran an article, "The Enteric Nervous System" by Raj K. Goyal and Ikuo Hirano, which posits the enteric nervous system (ENS) is a set of neurons that independently control the gastrointestinal tract from your central nervous system. It's amazing to stop and consider that anxiety isn't just in the mind, like in Short's case with eggs causing her anxiety.

The brain does not have a monopoly of stress' localization, which means you can't focus *only* on changing your thoughts if you want to resolve your stress. Getting the root cause requires thinking about how your entire body can holistically contribute to stress. When you start pushing the different levers of changes in diet and lifestyle, talk therapy and medication (with a doctor), meditation, and many more things I cover throughout this book, those activities can reduce the stress in your mind. Creator of Bulletproof Coffee, Dave Asprey, shares in an interview with Jim Kwik for his blog *Kwik Brain* that your brain can create new neural connections, a property researchers call "neuroplasticity." He says any age you can also create new healthy neurons via neurogenesis.

For most of us, it's easier to look at stress and mental health diagnoses and assume they're genetic and fixed. However, when we're willing to get a little uncomfortable and consider how our thoughts and behaviors could be contributing to or even creating these issues in our lives, we don't have to accept negative stress and anxiety as unchangeable. As I share in the introduction to this book, I found my anxiety and workplace stress wasn't just coming from external stimuli in the office. It was also coming from triggers I had carried since being hospitalized at age twelve. Events and circumstances had shaped me into having an anxious response. When we know what the root issues are, we're in a powerful situation to work with our body and mind to change the response.

The implications for stress and anxiety go much further than their external manifestations that affect our bodies and behavior. The science of anxiety shows us stress can also have an impact on your overall health. The body's design includes a set of automatic responses to deal with stress. Experiencing stress for extended periods (such as lower level but constant stressors at work) will activate your stress response, which may not get the chance to turn off. As you might imagine, having a constant, even low-grade, level of stress has consequences.

The Canadian Centre for Occupational Health Safety published a document, "OSH Answers Fact Sheets: Workplace Stress—General," which suggests unchecked stress can weaken your immune system, prevent you from sleeping, raise your blood sugar, raise your blood pressure, and increase the amount of cholesterol and fatty acids in your blood. They find stress can harm your social life by making you more anxious, restless, irritable, defensive, and angry. It can damage your work life by preventing you from thinking clearly or focusing on tasks. So, not only can stress make us less healthy, but it can also make us worse at our jobs, which can then feed back into existing insecurities and keep the cycle in place. Or we can interrupt it. I'm not telling you all of this to stress you out further (which you may be feeling right now reading this) but to tell you the urgency in which you need to address this issue. Well, guess what? You've come to the right place.

CONCLUSION

The next time you feel stress or anxiety, ask yourself what the stressors could be within your workplace and your world and find the root cause (don't forget the egg story). Like Short did, if possible, I suggest taking this journey with a mental health professional by your side. Stress can be unpleasant in the mind and have serious negative effects on your physical health, especially when it becomes anxiety and is not addressed for long periods. In the next chapter, I share holistic measures anyone can take to reduce stress and anxiety, many of which you might be surprised are more physical than mental. *Your physical health has a significant impact on your mental health.*

CHAPTER THREE

HOLISTIC STRATEGIES FOR STRESS MANAGEMENT

In the pursuit of writing this book, I had the pleasure of sitting (virtually) with Adrian France who cofounded her company, Odyssey, at the age of twenty-one. Odyssey started as a weekly newspaper at Indiana University as a way for her and her cofounder to connect with their peers to share information and opinions so those outside of the campus newspaper could also have a voice. It took off like wildfire, and they knew they needed to create a digital platform for the world to use. Odyssey transformed into a millennial social content platform that democratizes content to bring new, meaningful ideas to the world while enabling businesses to build relationships with more engaged audiences.

Sounds great, right? But expanding her business so quickly came at a cost. As a young cofounder, she experienced a lot of stress and pressure trying to balance the startup alongside her schoolwork and social life. As the company grew, so did France's responsibilities: "In early 2016, I shifted my focus to internal and external marketing for the organization, building Odyssey's brand in the market, proprietary events of over 50–250 people, sponsorship and partnerships, building strategic relationships with brands and agencies, as well as speaking and attending over forty industry events in 2016 alone." She found it exhilarating, but the workload was overwhelming.

Behind the scenes, overworking was taking a toll on her physically and mentally. She says, "It's hard when your influencers, mentors, or colleagues are constantly needing more and more from you with tighter and tighter deadlines, and as hard as you want to press on and think you can, your body is telling you otherwise." Personally, I've never been in as much of a high-pressure situation as this, but I certainly related to her circumstances where her productivity was scrutinized. As she puts it, "not being able to cut it was looked at as weakness." She didn't imagine stress and anxiety could or should be managed instead of being intrinsic parts of entrepreneurship.

As France continued to push hard for her company's success, she began to compromise her health. She says, "... when you get out of work at 2 a.m. and are working eighteen or more hours a day, there is no salad bar open, and you just end up eating fast food or what you can grab, so I gained weight." With such a grueling work schedule, there also wasn't time to exercise or even sleep properly. If she wasn't working, work was still on her mind, and she felt guilty to be doing anything else. As she reflects, "My productivity was lowest when I wasn't feeling well or taking care of myself." At a turning point, her hair stated falling out, and she was diagnosed with anxiety and prescribed a medication. We discussed whether this had ever happened to her before. She shared although she'd always felt anxiety, when her diet, sleep and stress got out of her control, she felt triggered to the point it was no longer manageable without help.

In addition to taking anxiety medication, France changed her lifestyle. Each day, she spent time away from screens and did healthy activities like meditating, taking a walk, or working out, as well as eating foods that would create and sustain energy throughout the day. After just thirty days of eating clean, she saw dramatic changes in her stress levels and sleep quality. "When I took care of myself, I was clearer. That brain fog was gone, and I was more productive, a better colleague, and more aligned with their ideas and mission of the company," she reflects. By 2021, Odyssey's platform was showcasing hundreds of thousands of articles with tens of millions of unique visitors each month

As I explained in the last chapter, there is an intimate bond entangling your physical and mental health. If you want to improve your mental health, a significant first step is to improve your physical health. This chapter demonstrates how the pillars of good health, diet, exercise, and sleep will help reduce your stress. These steps do not just focus on the problem of workplace stress. They help reduce all kinds of stress, including that of the workplace. After all, you bring your body to work with you. If you bring a tired, unhealthy body fueled by junk into work, you are not doing yourself any favors. Instead, you can bring a healthy, well-fueled, and rested body to work and you will be able to handle workplace stressors in a healthier way.

EAT WELL FOR LESS STRESS

Key elements of physical health—including diet—have a massive impact on stress and mental health, as abundant scholarly literature shows. In fact, as researchers Michael J. Gonzalez and Jorge R. Miranda-Massari write in their 2014 *Psychiatric Clinics of North America* article "Diet and Stress," "unhealthy foods, including 'refined carbohydrates, excessive animal fats, artificial colors, preservatives, and sweeteners,' could be considered stressors in and of themselves." *Wow.* We think of stressors as things like deadlines and dreaded activities, but they can also be food. "Unhealthy eating patterns will only result in an increased level of stress, followed by further health problems in the near future," the researchers conclude. Now, that's food for thought.

Fortunately, the article goes on to say we can prevent and even reverse these food stress effects. With a healthy eating plan accompanied with scientific supplementation and a proper stress management program, one can overcome stress, prolong one's life span, and reduce the likelihood of stress-related illnesses (Gonzales, 2014).

However, having a good diet is not only about avoiding bad foods; it is also about eating good food and supplementing that with vitamins. Gonzalez and Miranda-Massari suggest focusing on a Mediterranean diet, for instance, "consisting of increased levels of vegetables, fruit, whole grain, nuts, seeds, beans, eggs, and higher levels of fiber along with lower levels of red meats." They found vitamin supplements, like B vitamins, vitamin C, and magnesium supplements, were also shown to decrease stress. I personally find magnesium supplements to be particularly effective.

There is also a connection between digestion and anxiety. When we are in an anxious state, we go into fight or flight mode, and the energy that would have gone toward digestion goes elsewhere—like into your muscles—so you can survive. People cannot metabolize their food well then. To make things worse, many of us tend to eat more and choose foods that can be stressors when we're already feeling tension.

When people are anxious or stressed, many resort to food for comfort. Ahem, I'm guilty of this—cue the Oreo McFlurry. An occasional treat is okay, but if you feel like you are dependent on food for relief or are eating in excess, you may be seeking it to address your underlying anxiety and stress. Many of us reached for comfort foods during the pandemic. Remember in the initial panic of March 2020 many grocery stores were running out of bread and pasta but had plenty of spinach and carrots (Bin Zarah, 2020). This temporary food Band-Aid to numbing pain and stress is just another way of avoiding the real causes of anxiety, and when food is your stress management tool of choice, you're creating an unhealthy relationship with food and it's a clear sign you need to make a change.

I love to eat junk food and used to justify it by saying, "I deserve this," to myself after a long day. I kept eating ice cream, chocolate, and sugary drinks. Then I would feel guilty about what I ate later. Finally, I decided if I was going to make unhealthy food choices, then I needed to just accept them and not feel guilty. I said to myself, "Dude, if you're going to have the treat, then have the damn treat and don't feel guilty about it because then you ruin it. If you are going to feel guilty, then maybe don't eat the treat." I also started challenging myself to a month here and there of no processed sugar, which has raised my awareness of how much I used to rely on food to destress. I always drag my husband to join me in these monthly challenges, which helps me stay on track, and he grudgingly admits he feels better when he eats healthier, too.

One easy change to make is to eat intentionally instead of eating mindlessly. Instead of eating whatever is easiest and convenient, plan your meals in advance to make sure they are balanced and nutritious. Don't eat at your desk; instead, take an actual lunch break and have food you enjoy, eating away from your workplace. Do some calming techniques that get your body back to a relaxed state before eating, and when you do eat, eat with awareness of each bite and how it tastes and feels—at a reasonable pace. When you eat quickly, you activate a stress response in your body. Eating slowly has an additional benefit because it takes twenty minutes for your body to realize it is full. Accordingly, if you eat quickly, you may eat more than you need.

So, you can eat for less stress by choosing foods that aren't themselves stressors, avoiding mindlessly reaching for food when you're already stressed or anxious, and eating in a calm, focused way. As a bonus, you'll enjoy your meals more, feel lighter, and maybe even lose a pound or two. These de-stressing effects are further compounded when you add healthy movement into your lifestyle.

MOVE YOUR BODY, FEEL BETTER

What does "exercise" mean to you? We often think exercise has to mean dressing to go out and sweating for hours in a gym, which for many of us is not an appealing thought. Maybe the very idea of running for miles is itself a stressor, especially when you don't want to "waste" time working out instead of getting things done at work, as in France's case. However, what if we look at "exercise" a bit differently? For decreasing workplace stress, the simple practice of going for a walk or getting other light forms of exercise during your lunch break can make a significant impact.

In 2020, *Mayo Clinic Healthy Lifestyle* ran an article, "Exercise and Stress: Get Moving to Manage Stress," that shows how exercise can reduce stress. They argue:

"Virtually any form of exercise, from aerobics to yoga, can act as a stress reliever . . . because exercise releases endorphins, reduces the adverse physical effects of stress, improves mood, and [lowers] symptoms of mild depression and anxiety."

While this advice is not particularly groundbreaking, it is a fundamental truth about stress and anxiety: you will have less stress and anxiety and be better at dealing with stressors if you regularly exercise. Find a form of exercise that works for you and stick to it. You may be amazed at the results. My favorite kind of workout is to dance like nobody's watching! The key is to find something you enjoy so you will stick with it whether that be running, yoga, Pilates, strength training, or cycling.

Here's another reason to move your body. Amanda Daley's article "Exercise and Depression: A Review of Reviews" in *Journal of Clinical Psychology in Medical Settings* indicates exercise is a recommended form of treatment for mild depression. According to the authors of the meta data study she references, physical activity is "as effective as traditional interventions in some instances." You can improve your physical and mental health at the same time with exercise. As psychologists Michael Otto and Jasper Smits summarize in *Exercise for Mood and Anxiety: Proven Strategies for Overcoming Depression and Enhancing Well-Being*, exercise decreases anger, relieves some symptoms of anxiety and depression, and reduces the impact of several psychiatric disorders, including anxiety disorders.

I've personally found exercise can help relieve my GAD, and it's an important part of my holistic strategy to feel better. When I was pregnant with Rayaan, I went to the YMCA and took Zumba and boxing classes to regulate my anxiety around having a baby. I even obtained a yellow belt when I was thirty-six weeks pregnant. Then fast forward about two years later, when the pandemic hit, I couldn't go to the gym anymore.

At that time, I was pregnant with my second child and couldn't work out as much as before. To exercise from home, I got a Peloton stationary bike that includes live, virtual cycling classes. I would do twenty minutes on the Peloton for a fast, hard workout while still having the convenience of being at home. The endorphins released during exercise made me feel better and made me feel good because I did something beneficial for my body. After all, our body is a temple, isn't it? Taking care of myself helps relieve some anxiety. I notice when I do not add some movement to my day, I may be more on edge and easily agitated. Working out makes me feel better about myself and increases my energy even when I'm sleep-deprived with a toddler and a baby.

It just makes sense that exercise makes me feel less stress. Otto and Smits explain how exercise's benefits can go a step further and help you form resilience against stressors: "Exercise itself is a stressor . . . this sort of regular, planned stress may help your body be better at handling stress more generally. Your body is toughened up by exercise." Over time, exercise doesn't just help us manage the stress in a particular moment, but it can also help us feel less stress when those moments arise because we're more resilient.

Another meta-study by U. M. Kujala in *British Journal of Sports Medicine* conducted in 2009 summarizes additional impressive benefits of exercise including improving your breathing ability, making your muscles stronger, helping you fight sickness more effectively, and reducing pain caused by certain diseases. The American Heart Association (AHA) recommends exercising 90–150 minutes per week. Though everyone has their own definition of exercising, the AHA recommends hitting a heart rate 75 percent of your target maximum (220 minus your age) during your workout (Albert et al., 2019). Not only will this improve your cardiovascular system and keep your mind at ease, but you will also feel yourself burning off fat. So long and farewell, McFlurry!

If I've convinced you to give exercise another try, a simple rule I follow is to start slow and start small. Starting at ten minutes and increasing by one minute per day is better than working out for two hours once every two weeks. Bravo if you already have a regular exercise routine and now have an additional reason to stick to it.

Even for readers who are unable to start a new exercise regimen, you can introduce physical activity into your work life. In *Micro-Resilience: Minor Shifts for Major Boosts in Focus, Drive, and Energy*, Bonnie St. John and Allen P. Haines recommend an exercise they call the heart opener: "Sit at the edge of your chair, reach behind you and grab the back of the seat with both hands. Inhale and puff out your chest, arching your back." Other exercises, like shoulder rolls, toe lifts, and neck stretches, and being aware of your posture can quickly increase your sense of well-being at work. A stand-up desk is also a great way to encourage yourself to get moving. I used to have a stand-up desk at my old job, and to be honest, I would often forget to use it. However, I started setting reminders on my laptop to stand up intermittently throughout the day and that helped considerably. Get up and get that blood pumping to help improve your energy levels and mood.

SLEEP WELL

How many hours of sleep do you get on an average night? Sleep is another fundamental building block of good health and can have a beneficial impact on stress. In France's story, she was getting very little sleep in between the eighteen hours of work a day. Thinking about stressors can keep us awake when the lights are out or wake us up throughout the night, and we might also neglect our sleep to put in a few more hours of work. Maybe it seems like there's no real harm as long as you're getting to work on time.

The cost to our health and stress levels when we don't get enough restful sleep is eye-opening. The American Psychological Association conducted a sleep study and published their findings on their website in the article, "More Sleep Would Make Most Americans Happier, Healthier and Safer." According to the study, "Failing to get enough sleep dramatically impairs memory and concentration while increasing levels of stress hormones and disrupting the body's normal metabolism." Once again, there is a clear relationship between work being more difficult—for instance if you struggle to remember things and concentrate—and these factors that can increase stress in those moments, and all this can be mitigated with better sleep.

I found lack of sleep was a huge anxiety trigger for me. When I wouldn't get enough sleep, I would feel anxious and off the next day. When I had an anxiety disorder, I would worry about not having enough sleep or not being able to fall asleep, which would cause me to stay awake even longer. I would worry if I didn't get eight hours of sleep, I would experience a panic attack the next day. Now, even if I don't get eight hours and only get two or three hours of sleep, I no longer worry about having a panic attack. I may be groggy, but I get through the day, and I will be totally fine. To get to this point, I learned to change my response to lack of sleep or concerns when I experience anxiety.

Lack of sleep can slow you down at work in more ways than one. Michael Irwin writes in "Partial Night Sleep Deprivation Reduces Natural Killer and Cellular Immune Responses in Humans," published in *The FASEB Journal*, a lack of sleep can also decrease your immune function, making it more likely you'll get sick more frequently. Sickness itself can be a stressor, and it could also take you away from work, decreasing your productivity and increasing the stress you feel from stressors like deadlines. If you miss out on sleep, P.J. Rogers suggests in a September 2006 article in *Appetite* you may find yourself reaching for stimulants such as caffeine, which can increase anxiety. When I trimmed caffeine from my diet down to decaffeinated tea and coffee with trace amounts of caffeine, I noticed a huge improvement in my sleep quality. I stopped feeling on edge or jittery. Switching to decaf was a major game-changer for me.

Getting a good night's sleep can improve your mood, boost your immune health, and ameliorate symptoms of depression. A better night's sleep might reduce stressors, in turn reducing your stress. Also, a friendly reminder: if you are having a significant lack of sleep or high amounts of sleep that may be negatively affecting your way of life, this could be a sign of an underlying disorder (mental or physical). Be sure to check with your physician.

My suggestion for improving your sleep is to look at your sleep hygiene. You may be aware of dental hygiene or hand hygiene, but there is a whole world of sleep hygiene that goes unnoticed by most of us. I approach sleep hygiene in two parts: 1) the winding down phase and 2) the sleep phase.

The winding down phase entails creating the best circumstances for the sleep phase. All day, the less caffeine you intake, the better for your sleep phase. In addition to that general guideline, I focus my winding down on the last two hours before I got to bed. During this time, I turn off the TV, avoid exercise, and put away my smartphone. This first phase is part of my sleep schedule, followed by the sleep phase.

Some of you might have trouble falling asleep for the second phase. If this is the case, consider a few sleep strategies that have worked for me. One way to fall asleep is to practice total body relaxation. Starting at your feet and working your way up to your head, tighten your muscles for five seconds and then relax them. Work your way through all of your muscles while taking deep, even breaths. Another strategy I like is to simply count your breath. Keep a mental monologue going: "Inhale one, exhale one. Inhale two, exhale two." Once you get to exhale ten, start counting backward, repeating the process until you fall asleep.

If strategies like these don't work, you might consider using a white noise machine or listening to sleep stories or guided meditations. Apps like Calm and Headspace come preloaded with relaxing audio, gentle stories, and white noise to help you fall asleep. The guided meditations are great because you can focus on the audio instead of getting lost in your thoughts.

ADRIAN FRANCE WITH HER THREE PILLARS IN PLACE

Once Adrian France began to take control of her health, she began to feel less stress and improved her health. As part of her healing journey, she decided to take a sabbatical to figure out what she wanted to do after Odyssey. She realized she had a passion for helping entrepreneurs, seeing them grow and succeed both professionally and personally. She told me, "Entrepreneurs are a different breed, and the traditional world hasn't exactly set us up for success. . . . When you seek out advice from other entrepreneurs you see the one-hundred-hour work week glorified, that if you get more than four hours sleep, you don't want it enough." Now, she's committed to showing business owners there's a healthier way to also be more successful and avoid a cycle of "burnout, recovery, repeat."

As a start-up strategist, France focuses on the entrepreneur as a whole, their business, and themselves as a human, but you don't have to be a business owner or entrepreneur to learn from her example of workplace stress and its human toll. From France's story, it seems clear the pressures and stresses affecting entrepreneurs (and over-worked professionals whose work hours are not capped as they are loaded with projects and deadlines), can result in unhealthy and unsustainable work practices. She leaves us with this thought: "There will always be more work to do. Not everything is an emergency or a fire that needs to be addressed immediately. . . . If we aren't well, our business isn't well, and you can't pour from an empty cup."

CONCLUSION

The three fundamental components of good physical health—diet, exercise, and sleep—will go a long way toward improving your symptoms of stress. While these strategies are not panaceas, and they won't fix all of your problems, they are a great place to start. A wealth of scientific research backs them up, and versions of these strategies were mentioned by nearly every expert I spoke to in the process of researching and interviewing for this book. France found this balance by focusing on her healthy habits. Yet, adopting healthy habits is not the only strategy you can use to address your stress or anxiety. In the next chapter, I discuss another well-researched way of dealing with stress: therapy.

CHAPTER FOUR

THERAPY: MENTAL HEALTH MATTERS

What is one of your worst fears? Losing a loved one is one of mine, and right behind that is a loved one getting into a car accident. What does it feel like when one of your worst fears comes to fruition? Well, I found out four weeks after my second baby, Amira, was born in 2021 when I got a call from my husband. "I got into a car accident," my husband's words echoed in my head. These were words I always dreaded to hear; my worst fear just happened. Tears were running down my face as my son called for me from his highchair. I was in the middle of feeding him breakfast. Even when your worst fear happens, you have to keep being a mom because life doesn't stop for anyone.

My husband got into a high-speed collision on the highway during a snowy morning and thank God it wasn't his fault. The car was totaled, and all the airbags went off. I had to go pick up our belongings at the salvage yard. As I checked in, the man at the front desk looked at me with a concerned look and furrowed eyebrows, "Is your husband okay? Looked like it was a brutal accident." I sighed, "Yes, thank God he is okay." The man let out a sigh of relief. The man walked me to the car and as we got closer, I could feel my heart pounding. I was so nervous to see the car. "There it is," he said as he pointed to the wrecked car. Right then, as I saw the car, I just burst into tears. I saw images of my husband Omar in the car as he spun out of control. I saw all the airbags go off, an ambulance rush over, and the EMT help him out of the car. I saw it all in front of my eyes. I felt so much love in my heart for my husband, for what he had just been through and the pain he must be currently enduring.

Needless to say, Omar expressed his worries to me, that he had so much to lose, a wife and two kids, who depended on him. We also felt so much gratitude that although the accident was bad physically and mentally, at least he was still alive. We focused on being grateful and taking it day by day, which helped us get through this very difficult time.

My husband started therapy for PTSD after the car accident. In the end, my husband's left hand was fractured, and surgery was required. They put screws and plates in his hand, and he couldn't use it for eight weeks. Meanwhile, I had to take care of my newborn and a toddler. All this was stressful for me as a caregiver, and it took a toll on my husband's mental health not being able to help me and needing to process the shock, pain, and changes in his life that happened because of the accident.

He told me I could include his story in the book because men tend to think mental illness and anxiety is a sign of weakness. In reality, getting help is a sign of strength and shows the bravery and courage to deal with deep emotions and keep going.

If you are skeptical about pursuing therapy for your stress or anxiety, you're not alone. I was hesitant when I was first advised to undergo therapy after the disastrous work performance evaluation in the introduction to this book. Up to that point, I thought it would be enough to talk to my friends and family about my problems.

Finally, faced with losing my job if I didn't find a way to manage my anxiety, I started weekly therapy and was reading self-help books. As I worked with the therapist, I noticed how she asked me questions instead of just telling me her opinion or what she would do in my shoes. Instead, she would ask questions about my feelings and thoughts, waiting patiently for me to decide how I felt and what I wanted to do. No matter what I told her, she never judged me, and I didn't feel like I had to say what she wanted to hear or expected. In contrast, I realized my well-intentioned friends and family do not have the years of education and training mental health professionals do, nor are they non-judgmental. I hadn't been opening up fully and honestly about my feelings with people I felt safe and comfortable with because I was concerned about their opinions of me. Not so much with the therapist.

Therapists are great because you can tell them anything and everything. They don't judge (and if they do, who cares?), they are great listeners, and they are highly trained in many therapeutic models so they can properly diagnose and treat you. In an article published in *Frontiers in Psychology* in October 2011, Researchers Rita B. Ardito and Daniela Rabellino wrote about the relationship between therapist and patient. They suggested the therapeutic alliance between patient/client and therapist is really important, no matter what kind of therapy you use.

In addition to cognitive behavioral therapy and talk therapy, there are many different types of therapies, and most therapists are trained in more than one modality. It's important to be open with your therapist about what is or isn't working to ensure you are receiving the most appropriate treatment. I have tried and benefited from many mental health therapies including CBT, biofeedback, regular talk therapy, and hypnotherapy. I found all of them to be very helpful at different times and in specific ways. Your therapist will help you find the therapy that's right for you. In this chapter, I share stories from others who found help with workplace stress and anxiety through different therapies as well as those from my own life.

NOT DEALING WITH IT YOURSELF

Christopher Weber, an intellectual property attorney and retired lieutenant commander with the US Navy Reserve, agreed to speak with me about his workplace stress and ways he coped with it. During his time in the US Navy Reserve, he revealed there were moments of workplace stress while in high-performance intense environments. "I dealt with it myself," he said. When he returned to civilian life and became a lawyer, the stress became constant, and what he had done on his own to de-stress before wasn't working as well for him.

He felt the pressures of trying to get a job in a big law firm and then working to gain partnership in the firm. Meanwhile, as he puts it, "I [would] see people who have been amazing at everything all their life, really smart and qualified people, and they get fired.... The work world is a very competitive place, and there's a lot of pressure to be the best, so it breeds anxiety." The law firm was the ultimate pressure cooker.

This went on for years. He told me the stress became debilitating, and I asked in what ways. The answer may sound familiar to some readers. Almost every night, he slept with his phone beside his bed. Each time he looked at the phone, he couldn't just leave it there. He said, "I felt compelled to pick it up and see if anything came in, even in the middle of the night, and even if I tried to ignore emails, I couldn't stop thinking about it until I addressed them." Even if he tried to take a vacation, he would continue to check his email and do work remotely.

To address this problem, Weber took two steps: first, he left that high-pressure workplace for a lower-pressure job. Second, he started seeing a therapist. Weber believes speaking with the therapist was an important step in overcoming his anxiety. He told me, "Even if I'm in good physical shape, nobody would think it's crazy if I got a personal trainer, and so seeing a therapist is similar. It's like seeing a trainer for your mind." That is such a good analogy, and in the same line of thought that we're often encouraged to see a doctor before starting a new workout routine or weight loss plan, it's important to first see a mental health professional to address stress and anxiety. In both cases, those professionals can address root causes and pitfalls we can't see.

On the value of therapy, Weber says, "It's not always clear why we are feeling anxious, and therapy can help those suffering from anxiety determine the causes." He also agrees with the value of talking to someone who's not judgmental and whom you don't have a personal relationship with. The advantage is, as he puts it, "They don't have a reason to tell you something you want to hear and can help you learn . . . how to deal with your anxiety."

BECOMING YOUR OWN THERAPIST

Her glucose levels dropped, her blood sugar dropped, and her blood pressure spiked. This was Hania's first panic attack, and it happened at work at a nonprofit in Washington, DC. She told me in an interview that she suddenly found herself sitting on the floor hyperventilating because that was all she could physically do. She was upset, crying, and could not breathe. Hania had no idea what was going on or how to make it stop. She described the attack as, "so physical and so intense [it felt like] my body had given up on me." A coworker had to call an ambulance.

This was a breaking point. She had studied international relations in college as she planned to work at an international non-governmental organization. However, in the three years of her first job, she was not given the respect or opportunities she deserved. As a South Asian woman, she endured microaggressions and racist comments in the workplace. She tried to take initiative and combat the racism by being active in company organizations such as the leadership association. In this association, she voiced what was happening to her. Yet she was ultimately rejected by the people she spoke out to. They claimed this wasn't an issue because her experiences were personal to her. Oh, and they claimed that microaggressions and racist comments don't happen to everyone. *That's the whole idea.*

The harassment went beyond words and into actions. Some of Hania's coworkers and managers became unsatisfied with her qualifications. Her managers hired applicants with fewer skills and degrees for the positions she was aspiring to get. She was told over and over again she ultimately could not achieve her goal of getting into programmatic work. She even started to believe this herself. Hania felt like a failure. She felt stuck and alone but did not ask for help. This was when her anxiety began to worsen, and she had her first panic attack. The frightening experience showed her she needed to leave that job for the sake of her mental wellbeing.

Unfortunately, Hania faced the same problems at her new job. When she would wake up in the morning, she would feel sheer dread at the thought of going to work. She would come home exhausted and knowing she had tried her best but would never be truly appreciated for it. She felt overwhelmingly sad. She stopped eating as much, stopped hanging out with friends, and focused on work. Her apartment had become a huge mess, which her family noticed because she wasn't normally messy. Her environment was mirroring the chaos she felt.

She finally decided to go to therapy and get some insight into what was going on in her mind. Enter, therapy. Hania explained a huge part of her healing was learning through her therapist that she cannot control what other people say or do, but she can control her reactions. This caused her to realize she would get triggered by certain things, like if she did not meet others' expectations, she would feel like a failure. Therapy helped her realize she should focus on more important questions: What were her expectations for herself? What were her goals for herself? Putting herself and her goals above others was a key part of her healing process.

The kind of therapy that helped her understand her triggers and helped interrupt her thought-patterns is cognitive-behavioral therapy (also called CBT). There is an enormous amount of evidence showing CBT is effective against a number of mental health issues. As Butler notes in a January 2006 article in the *Clinical Psychology Review*, CBT is "substantially superior to wait list or no-treatment controls, nondirective therapy, and pill placebo." CBT is also a remarkably robust way to deal with panic disorders according to the study. Additionally, the effects of CBT used to treat panic disorders are lasting. Indeed, Hania was able to reclaim her mental health with this therapy.

It wasn't always an easy road, though. Speaking about mental health is not encouraged in the South Asian community. Therefore, after her panic attack experience and after admitting her anxiety, her family and friends treated her as sensitive and fragile. She wanted them to know, "I'm not a broken, shattered piece of glass, and I don't want to be treated like one. I'm an intellectual and intelligent person who has many accolades and accomplishments." In her healing, she has emphasized that her accomplishments and intelligence, not her anxiety, define her.

Since starting therapy, she has made a great deal of progress toward managing her anxiety. She realized anywhere she goes, she might deal with a bad situation, so she must work on herself to a point where those incidents will not bother her anymore. Now, she is stronger, more resilient, and more confident in herself. Additionally, Hania is learning the tools of CBT to understand her anxiety and pinpoint what triggers her so she can be her own therapist.

I was very interested to hear how she utilizes her Islamic religious beliefs to tap into her mental health. To do so, she looked up stories of how specific Muslim role models have dealt with stress. She mentions prophets she read about, such as Yunus (Yousef) and Muhammad (peace be upon him). Through YouTube videos that focus on mental health and Islam, she was able to connect herself more deeply to her religion. It made her religion deeper and more purposeful for her. "The role faith has played in my anxiety is the grounding I definitely needed." Her faith reminded her of the bigger picture of reality, helping her realize everything and every problem is not the end.

RESISTANCE TO THERAPY

Often, finding the therapy you need can be challenging. One person I interviewed, Deyanah, described the social and familial barriers to therapy she faced. As a young woman, she experienced a severe anxiety attack and realized she needed help. She asked her parents about going to therapy, but both her parents did not think she needed it. They did not believe in therapy and the healing effects behind it. This disappointment led Deyanah to feel anger and resentment because she was not getting the help she needed, and she felt even worse. Finally, she found the courage to start going to therapy without her parents' support.

She described therapy as "life changing." When I asked her how so, she had plenty to say. Deyanah was finally able to talk in a safe space with someone who listened to her and wanted to know why she felt the way she did. She found a space where she was not told to shut down her feelings. Instead, she explored those feelings. She emphasized the importance of forming a bond with your therapist since without a connection, it is difficult to get to the root of your worries. This makes sense because if you don't feel the therapist cares, you won't want to answer hard questions or think about difficult topics with them. With that bond, you also have an excellent foundation for therapy to work, as it did for her.

She referred to therapy as a "mental gym" and said, "I go to the gym, I work out, I eat pretty clean, and [I] like to stay healthy. So why have I been neglecting my brain for so long? None of that other stuff matters if your mental health is just not there." This comment reminds me of Weber, who said something very similar to me about therapy being like hiring a personal trainer. Spending time, money, and effort to improve our mental health should be as normal as those activities are for improving physical fitness.

Therapy changed her perspective and how she sees and reacts to circumstances in her daily life in many ways. She allows herself to think and process now. Most importantly, she has learned to face her problems head-on rather than ignore them. Additionally, she has learned to ease her anxiety with tools her therapist suggested. One habit she has picked up is setting reminders to eat, drink water, and take a minute to think about herself. This reminder ensures she is taking care of herself mentally and physically. All of these habits and lessons have made her more self-aware.

Deyanah also learned how to set boundaries in her life—especially with her family. With the help of her therapist, she was able to successfully communicate these boundaries and set them, resulting in relief from her stress at home. Amazingly, her mother was touched by the positive effects of this therapy and now believes in and fully supports it.

LOOKING FEAR IN THE FACE

I had many different fears come and go through the nine years I experienced an anxiety disorder. At one point, for about a year, I had a fear of flying. It happened out of nowhere one day after my sister and I had boarded a plane for a five-hour flight. We were sitting on the plane waiting to take off; I was exhausted that day and hadn't gotten much sleep the night before. It was a night flight, so it was dark, and the interior of the plane started getting warm. We waited for over an hour to take off because of some airplane traffic. I began to panic. My chest felt tight, my legs started shaking, and my heart raced; I had a panic attack. I just wanted to get off the plane. I wanted to tell the flight attendant to turn around and let me off, but I knew I couldn't do that.

I had flown thousands of times ever since I was a baby. I *loved* flying! As a kid, I loved fourteen-hour flights. I would say, "I wish the flight were longer." I don't know what I was thinking, but it just goes to show you how much I loved flying. Now all of a sudden, because of that one time I had a panic attack on the plane, I was afraid of flying. My brain started to perceive flying as dangerous because of that one incident on the plane. The mind is funny that way. I started associating flying with panic. My brain made up many stories about how if it happened before, it would happen again, and how would I escape the plane if I had a panic attack?

Around this time, I started seeing a hypnotherapist to help me fly again fear-free. Alongside hypnosis, I underwent exposure therapy to overcome my fear of flying. Exposure therapy is a technique where the patient is exposed to the thing they fear in a safe setting. The more I flew and put myself in that situation and survived, the more my brain realized maybe it wasn't that dangerous after all. I became desensitized to the fearful sensations of flying and learned to accept them, sit with them, not react, practice deep breathing, and let the feelings and sensations pass. This was not easy at all, but it paid off.

Although initially, I saw the hypnotherapist to overcome my fear of flying, he helped me with more than that. The therapist encouraged me to dig into my past, face traumatic events, and resolve them. The thing they don't tell you about in therapy is when you face your traumatic event, it is quite painful and emotional at first, but that doesn't have to be the case forever.

My therapist told me I was clinging onto my anxiety from the hospitalization, which kept changing through the years. Once I would resolve one fear, I would develop a fear of something else. Another reason I was not letting go of my anxiety was because of a belief I had from when I was a child. Somewhere, I must have heard, "God tests those he loves the most," and, "God is closer to those who are suffering." Through many sessions of therapy, we finally got down to those deeply rooted beliefs I had. Then, my therapist asked me, "Do you think God wants you to be happy?" I replied excitedly, "Yes!" "Do you think God wants you to suffer?" I responded, "Of course not!" I was taught God is ever-loving, the most beneficial, merciful, and forgiving. Then, why was I forgetting what I knew of God's nature? Once I challenged those mistaken beliefs with the truth, I let my anxiety go.

Doing this healing work is like ripping a Band-Aid off. It hurts at first, but the wound needs oxygen to heal. To fully heal, you must face your inner demons and any past traumatic events. I cried a lot, especially during the first few therapy sessions, and I didn't always feel the best afterward. For a few years, whenever I discussed my hospitalization with ARDS, I would cry. However, after working through and processing those difficult times, I truly healed. Today, I don't get emotional when I talk about traumatic events. Now, I can freely talk about what happened to me, thanks to all the good therapy I received.

CONCLUSION

The stories you've read about above show the ways therapists help patients understand and combat stress and anxiety with real, tangible benefits. If you face social barriers to getting help, whether through your culture, gender, etc., I urge you to push past them. Do what you need to do to get the therapy you need. Don't feel discouraged if you don't see an improvement in your symptoms when you first begin therapy. Hang in there and stick with it. Sometimes you need a combination of therapies, so it may be a matter of trying different things until you find the mode of therapy that best fits your mental health challenges. With time you will see results. Trust me, therapy will change your life.

CHAPTER FIVE

DEVELOPING RESILIENCE

My dad, Dr. Hyder Alam, was shocked to see an FBI agent standing at the door of his medical practice office.

Talk about stress at work! Oh, and did I mention this was fall of 2001, right after 9/11? My father looks like a stereotypical Middle Eastern Muslim, so he was already feeling quite vulnerable about where he stood in American society. Knowing he had nothing to hide, my dad gladly answered all the questions about his travel history—which didn't include Afghanistan—lack of flight training, and never giving money to extremist groups. At the end of the interview, the FBI agent was satisfied there was no reason to investigate further.

They became so chummy that my dad asked, "If I may know, how was it I came to be reported?" The agent paused and said, "I think there's professional jealousy here." My dad was and still is bright and charismatic, and he exudes confidence and leadership qualities. His patients love him—well, everyone loves him—so it was not surprising someone may have been experiencing some professional jealousy.

Yet this was just one month before my dad was fired from his job. His hands were shaking as he read the letter of termination. The letter couldn't have come at a worse time. He was one month away from completing his three years of employment in the US to get his green card.

This should have been the end of a long journey that took him, my mom, Unsar Tahira, and their four children, Massoma, Monis, Mohammad, and Fathima (I'm the eldest), from the Punjab province of Pakistan to Iran, Ireland, and then a small town called Fredonia in New York. We moved every two years until I was twelve years old. With each immigration to a new country, my dad had to take the medical exams of the country and redo residency training, which he did without complaint. I give major props to my mom as well. She was in her early twenties, all alone in a new country where she didn't speak the language, raising children while her husband was busy trying to make a living for their family. I know this time was a very arduous time for my mom, but she held her head high and faced it like a trooper.

Living on a residency salary with four kids was also not easy. We experienced this in Ireland when we were so poor there sometimes wasn't enough heat in our home, but this was different. It wasn't just exploitative, it was illegal. He carefully reviewed his employment contract, which said if there was a conflict or other issues, they needed to resolve it themselves or have a lawyer to resolve it before they can terminate. He called his lawyer. Ultimately, the employer allowed my father to complete the final month of work, and then he was terminated. It was good he'd completed the three years of employment for the green card requirement, but as it must be processed and issued, he was still unemployed and unable to practice medicine.

My father's problems with his employer didn't end here, but over time they shifted. Even though our family's precarious permission to be in this country and the difficulty for my father to provide for us was incredibly stressful, his actual work was enjoyable, and he did find another job at a medical practice. Also, my father's patients loved him. He told me, "I got a lot of confidence from patients because they loved me and still wanted to be my patients."

I asked what it was that kept my father going during the hard times. For him, the worst-case scenario would have been to lose his job and have all his hard work getting to the United States end, then having to return to Pakistan as a failure. In reality, the worst-case scenario was one of his children becoming sick. He said when I was hospitalized with ARDS, *that* was the worst and most stressful time in his life. Not losing his job a month before he got his green card, not having an FBI agent come to his work, not the possibility he may lose everything and have to return to Pakistan—but it was watching his eldest daughter fighting for her life.

My dad made the point that above all else, family, life, and health are of far greater importance than any job. He said, "I think Allah was showing me what's really important in life . . . and I think if you have trust in yourself, you are not a mean person, and you don't have malicious thinking

... you will do well." I really feel my dad has life figured out. He doesn't sweat the small stuff, he lives life to the fullest, and he is always smiling and laughing. His energy is so contagious, and even if you are having the worst day, he will make you smile. If you ever meet my dad, you will know exactly what I am talking about. He has the best laugh. He always tells me to live life with love, lead with love, and just open your eyes to the beauty of the world.

Today my dad owns his medical practice, and his former employer actually came and made him an offer for a buyout. When my dad was in a position of authority over the people who had made his life so hard a decade before, he showed kindness and never brought up the past. That is resilience.

We've all been tested in many ways during the pandemic, both in our work and personal lives. These new stressful situations have also opened the possibility to practice our resilience. In this chapter, I start with small changes to create micro-resilience and then look at the role your positive attitude and relationships can play in your ability to manage stress.

DEVELOPING MICRO-RESILIENCE

Most of us wouldn't normally expect a five-year old child who has a leg amputated to go on to win two Olympic medals in skiing and be the first African-American to do so. That's just what Bonnie St. John, a bestselling author, keynote speaker, resilience ringleader, and Olympic medalist, did. I first met her at the TEDx speaker dinner the night before the event, and my husband and I enjoyed chatting with her and her husband, Allen Haines, who's been a marketing CEO and consultant to Disney, IMG, NBS/Universal, and Fox. The couple developed the concept of "micro-resilience," which was the subject of her talk—one of my favorites of the whole day. While writing this book, I contacted her and was delighted she agreed to an interview.

My first question was about why we need this idea of micro-resilience. She said, "A lot of leaders think you need to drive yourself until you drop, but that isn't the most productive way to get work done . . . [and] giving those who report to you stress isn't going to get their best work out of them." To get the best work possible, St. John recommends fostering micro-resilience which, as she said, "is teaching leaders how to get small recoveries along the way . . . to maximize focus, energy, and productivity." I reflected on my stressful experience with the nonprofit where I was working nonstop, and her way sounded much better.

She and Haines compiled their best ideas and research on high performance in their book, *Micro-Resilience: Minor Shifts for Major Boosts in Focus, Drive, and Energy*. They rethink today's prevalent "drive until you drop" philosophy and instead shift our focus onto small, immediately effective adjustments that allow people to be more resilient every hour, every day, all day long. As more and more of us are working from home some or all of the time, their tips are still very helpful for not burning out and doing your best work over the long term.

One part of the book that stands out to me is the research they cite from Dr. James Loehr, a performance psychologist and author of *The Power of Full Engagement*. He studied world-class tennis players to understand what makes them stand out from other top players and why only some champions consistently took home the trophies. Loehr did many different analyses but could not find any consistent differences between the best players. Then he noticed after scoring and between games and sets, the top tennis players were doing little things to recover which were focused on energy recovery and positive focus. These activities were found in the study to bring their heart rates back to normal faster than less successful players. As St. John and Haines say, "The small recoveries along the way, such as putting their racket in their other hand, positive self-talk, getting their heart rate down, and not paying attention to the audience, is what made these top players the winners." In other words, they were de-stressing themselves after the stressful moment had passed.

Loehr used these findings to revolutionize sports training with a program he calls The Sixteen-Second Cure, which is now the industry standard in tennis coaching. As St. John and Haines write, the program is "a series of focus exercises and relaxation techniques that teach players to shake off mistakes, release tension, project a confident image to their opponents, and establish rituals to increase consistency." Loehr's work inspired St. John and Haines to call these mini recoveries "micro-resilience" and to relate this idea to life in general, not just sports. What if what made the top tennis players rise to the top are the same patterns that can make all of us better perform in stressful situations?

There are five mini-recovery activities St. John and Haines recommend to speed up our daily recoveries during workplace stress or any other stressors. These activities correlate with content and stories I've included in this book and include:

1. Refocus your brain: Think, organize, and execute more effectively. My father did this when he got fired, then checked his contract, then called his lawyer.
2. Reset your primitive alarms: Stop your emotions from being hijacked. These include methods to deal with our fight-or-flight response, like how in the last chapter Hania uses CBT to reduce her panic attacks.
3. Reframe your attitude: Spiral into the positive. There's a great story of Jess Ruggieri using positive thinking to overcome stress later in this chapter.
4. Refresh your body: Increase your fuel efficiency. Review my health habit tips in Chapter Three to keep your body and mind in top performance mode.
5. Renew your spirit: Tap into the power of purpose. In Chapter Twelve I share tips for finding more purpose in your life and work.

Together, these activities build your micro-resilience through minor shifts you make throughout your day that yield major boosts in your energy and productivity (St. John, 2017).

Here's an example St. John shared with me in our conversation of how her client used micro-recovery activities. This client believes because her boss required her to answer quickly, she must, and everything needs her attention immediately because her coworkers count on her. I have felt this way before, and maybe you have, too. From St. John's perspective, work doesn't have to be this way, and she combines her refocus, reset, and reframe tools to help this client find a solution.

There are workarounds to address almost any challenge. St. John recommends you can arrange mutually acceptable expectations for email, text messages, and phone calls that let you do your best work, yet still be responsive to truly critical communications, as well as to the overall flow of information throughout your organization. Your boss will probably be flexible once he or she understands the diminishing returns that result from numerous disruptions. The possibilities are endless for how you can look at any stressors from work, run them through St. John's process, and find creative solutions that will reduce your stress with the added benefit of increasing your productivity.

It's important to remember your brain doesn't have an infinite capacity for decision-making or other cognitive activities. St. John leaves us with a useful decision-making strategy: "Make important decisions in the morning or after you have had food, rest, and something that makes you feel more positive because of decision fatigue. We tend to make more mistakes or poor decisions later in the day." The choice is in your hands. You can make the decision today to start implementing healthy habits to create a better life for yourself.

WHEN THE GOIN' GETS TOUGH—GET TOUGHER!

Jess Ruggieri is an employee engagement coordinator at the University at Delaware and former strategist with "the fun dept," a company that encourages playing at work to improve culture and enhance employee engagement. The reason I reached out to interview her wasn't just her happy approach to work. I wanted to know more about her personal story of how she came to be so positive and such a people-person.

Ruggieri grew up emotionally and physically separated from her parents, and she often relied on her friends' parents for support. As she puts it, "growing up as a child without feeling the sense of security . . . that can really like follow you into adulthood." Because of her childhood experiences, she would often find herself wondering, "If you don't take care of yourself, you could fall, you could fail, and who's there to catch you?" This lack of security paved the way for her to experience anxiety and find other sources of support.

The turning point in her life was on her eighteenth birthday as she was leaving home for the first time to attend college in Virginia. That day, she drove to Virginia with her mother and aunt, and it unfolded like this:

"We got in the car, we drove to Virginia, they dropped me off, we unpack my things, and literally right after, the next thing my mom said was, 'All right, well, it's going to get dark, so we have to get on the road soon.' So there I was, an eighteen-year-old on my birthday in this new place—alone."

After they left, she went to find her mailbox, and in it was a birthday card from her college advisor. It was confusing to her that this stranger sent her a card, yet her own mother had just left her, and she was at a fork in the road. She could choose to feel sad about her family neglecting her birthday or happy this new mentor remembered. She chose the positive, a choice that helped her start classes and learn instead of being distracted by personal chaos.

Ruggieri advises we try to take a positive outlook on even the negative things happening in our life so we can continue doing our work and making a positive impact on others. Genuinely caring for others ultimately leads to a more fulfilling and productive life, a sentiment both she and my dad would agree on. "My end goal is being my ultimate self to love people well.... If I'm wrapped up in my own junk ... then how can I be truly ... loving and caring for those around me?" At this point, she teared up, feeling her deep affection for others. It was a very powerful moment.

She's the kind of person who will see someone on the street and randomly think, "Do they know how loved they are? Do they know what a wonderful creation they are?" As she uttered these words, she became teary eyed. This also ties into her Christian faith about what her life's purpose is—to serve others. Her love for others and her faith are resilience super-chargers. When faced with adversity, she goes straight to looking for the positive and then trying to find a way this situation is part of her purpose. Ruggieri is also very finely tuned into her emotional needs and asks for help when she needs it instead of trying to fake it and act like nothing is wrong. But it's important to remain calm even in chaotic circumstances: "I just kind of refocus," she says, echoing St. John.

Sometimes it's tough to stay positive when hurtful or sad things happen, like losing a loved one or being treated unfairly at work as my dad was. In those times, it is often helpful to stay with those emotions, sit with them, and accept them. I often teach my kids "all feelings are welcome." However, staying positive didn't stop my dad from contacting a lawyer to stand up for himself. In fact, staying positive helped him fight for what he knew was right. This is the opposite of toxic positivity, which ignores your material reality and says you should be happy even in dire situations. The point here is no matter what happens, you can choose your outlook, and when it's positive, you are able to see opportunity even in unpleasant situations.

One of the fundamental building blocks of resilience is a sense of social connectedness, as Ruggieri discovered in her own experience. Fostering a sense of genuine and reciprocal social connectedness can help your mental health in a variety of ways, including increasing your resilience. As researchers Dennis S. Charney and Steven M. Southwick write in *Resilience: The Science of Mastering Life's Greatest Challenges*, "close relationships build strength and help to protect us during times of stress and danger. Far from signifying weakness, interdependence with others can provide a foundation for resilience." This is the strength Ruggieri found growing up when she looked to other trusted adults when her parents weren't there to support her. In your workplace structure or professional community, do you have close relationships? If not, this might be a great place to start building resilience. It could be as simple as my dad's fellow doctor who wrote him an encouraging letter during a difficult time.

Charney and Southwick tell the harrowing story of a group of Vietnam prisoners of war who bolstered their own resilience in horrifying prison conditions by clandestinely communicating with one another. They say you don't need to be in such a desperate situation for your resilience to be bolstered by social connection: having a support network can help you deal with stress and can prevent the development of symptoms of PTSD. As the authors argue, too, social support can improve physical as well as mental health.

Ruggieri's focus on giving to others is also supported by the research in *Resilience,* as it turns out, because giving social support helps with resilience as much as receiving social support, "perhaps equally so" (Charney, 2012). Focusing on reciprocal social relationships, as Ruggieri does, can be an extremely useful tool to increase resilience, including resilience to workplace-related stress. It can also improve your overall physical and mental health.

When I reflect on Ruggieri's almost defiant choice not to dwell on the negative, to find mentors and fulfill her life's purpose, I'm reminded of Idil Ahmed, author of *Manifest Now.* In a Twitter post in 2018, Ahmed said, "You can rise up from anything. You can completely recreate yourself... All that matters is that you decide today and never look back." Now, that's resilience.

CONCLUSION

My dad found resilience in the face of workplace discrimination because of his faith and determination to succeed for his family. This led him to be calm and even kind under stress, which created future opportunities for him that he hadn't even dreamt of at the time. St. John and Haines teach micro-resilience for executives and professionals to build strength to perform under pressure, in the form of mini activities to boost energy and speed recovery between stressful events. Ruggieri chooses to see the positive and build a support system she can lean on, which gives her resilience despite her parents not being there when she was growing up. Whatever might have been missing from your life or circumstances, you can overcome these things and succeed regardless. I speak more about this in the next chapter, which is about not bringing personal stress into the workplace.

CHAPTER SIX

BRINGING STRESS INTO THE WORKPLACE

When I was working at a nonprofit, even hearing a beeping sound would cause me to start feeling anxious. It reminded me of the hospital machines beeping several years ago. The thing is, in these moments, I didn't necessarily realize the relationship between my sudden anxiety, the beep, and the memory. Sometimes the stress and anxiety you feel at work can stem from unprocessed emotions around traumatic events in your past.

The old memory being called up was a life changing event. My family and I had gone to Philadelphia for vacation when I was a freshman in high school. We rode on a beautiful horse-drawn carriage, looking at the old city and colonial buildings. When we returned home to Buffalo, New York, we expected everything to go back to normal. A few days later, my temperature spiked to 104°F, and I was showing signs of dehydration. A few hours after being given an IV of fluids and being tested, the doctor said I could go home. Something in my gut said I should stay. I had a feeling something terrible was happening. So,

I told my parents to tell the doctors I would like to stay, and they kept me for observation.

Later that night, my condition worsened. I was having difficulty breathing and needed more oxygen. Because of my age, the doctors recommended I be transferred to the local children's hospital. I was terrified. A few hours ago, I had been told to go home. Now I was in an ambulance, being rushed to the nearest children's hospital, which was about an hour away. That feeling of fear and uncertainty—the experience of struggling with every breath—was excruciating, and I would not wish it upon my worst enemy. As the siren screamed, it pulled the breath from my lungs; my breathing was even more labored. An intense feeling of anxiety was now blinding me. I had never experienced anxiety like this before. I was in uncharted territory.

Once I arrived at the children's hospital, I screamed uncontrollably for my parents and my doctors to help me. They wheeled me away into the ICU. That was the last thing I remembered, then darkness.

I developed many fears from this hospitalization experience. I came to associate elements of this experience like the beeps from machines with life-and-death danger. The association of "beep equates fear" caused me to feel anxiety in a busy office with the copy machine going on constantly. In that way, I was bringing my old issues to the present workplace. Because I did it without awareness, there was no boundary for me between the old anxiety and the actual work to be done that day.

Highly traumatic incidents aren't the only ones we can carry into work. As I discuss with Santoshi Pattem in this chapter, people often hold a lot of limiting beliefs from past experiences that influence our present and future, and we need to be cognizant of those so we can move past them. Our family, our spouses, our past, influential people in our life, or our upbringing may influence our workplace issues. Many of us have new traumas from the effects of the COVID-19 pandemic, ranging from our or our loved ones' medical experiences and the uncertainty and changes in our society and homes as result. We bring all these personal stresses with us to work—even if it's to a remote desk.

Sometimes, the solution is to separate the past from the present to create a work-life balance, and at other times, it's about asking for help and not piling on guilt to an already difficult circumstance, such as for working moms. In other cases, the work stress might be telling you the workplace isn't a fit, and that's okay.

STRESS AND LIFE AT WORK

COMMON STRESSORS WE BRING TO WORK

There is no rigid boundary between workplace stress and other forms of stress. Santoshi Pattem knows this well. Pattem is a mindset coach who helps individuals embrace a positive and empowering relationship with work, and I interviewed her for this book. She shared a story about a client whose workplace stress was a result of stressors from outside the workplace. "A client came to me who had been having issues dealing with authority, and they were constantly worried about losing their job," she explained. She knew her role was to help the client answer the question, "Where is this stemming from?" The answer turned out to be issues in their past growing up in an authoritarian household. This wasn't the first time Pattem noticed stressors from outside the workplace affecting work performance.

She's worked with many clients experiencing divorces and legal issues and observed that, "It's inevitable we bring that stress to work, which affects our relationship with work." Since the work-life relationship is inevitable, we have to learn to navigate it. To help the client who couldn't handle feedback, Pattem said, "I worked with her to make her realize not all feedback from others should be taken so negatively, and we shouldn't see it as us being judged by our boss but more as a learning opportunity." This reframing of feedback allowed her client to receive the next performance evaluation neutrally, instead of from a defensive position, because she wasn't attaching her past experience to that present moment.

Family stress is not the only kind that can be brought to the workplace. You might be carrying some emotional baggage from a previous job. Pattem added employees working in a new role often "struggle because they had a set of skills and knowledge from their previous roles, and they can't quite adapt to the new organization." Because of this lack of adaptation, these employees might blame the job itself, their boss, or even their desk. Pattem asserts these employees need to "adjust to their new environment by thoroughly studying the organization and getting familiar with [its] culture." New employees might need to learn "the history of the organization, how people work and interact here, and how they can use their skills in this job." Pattem emphasized employees should understand their job and company's context and learn how to bring their skills and knowledge to their new position.

While Pattem was a strategic talent manager, her primary responsibilities were to onboard and train new employees. All of the employees came to the new job with knowledge, skills, and abilities. All of them also set expectations about what the job would be and how they would handle it. They assumed they would hit the ground running because they had done a similar position in another organization. They set false expectations for themselves and the company, which resulted in a lot of stress and demotivation. Pattem tells me, "Some of them would find it especially challenging to understand the context and change of environment in the new job, so they would either quit or suffer because of job stress."

SETTING A WORK-LIFE BALANCE

One way to address this source of workplace stress is to establish a sense of work-life balance. For many of us, work-life balance is elusive. The truth is sometimes life will be out of balance. For example, when starting a new job, you may need to put in more time and effort to show your worth and commitment. In contrast, when you have a newborn, you may be home more and spending more time with your family. These are the ebbs and flows of life, and it is expected. Furthermore, not everyone will be able to have a "work-life balance." It is a privilege even to be able to obtain that goal. Not everyone can afford childcare, and some people have to work three jobs to support their families.

So how can you establish a work-life balance? Ioana Lupu and Mayra Ruiz-Castro, a pair of business researchers, conducted almost two hundred interviews for *Harvard Business Review,* and they suggest taking stock of your life: "Ask yourself: What am I willing to sacrifice, and for how long? If I have been prioritizing work over family, for example, why do I feel that it is important to prioritize my life in this way? . . . What regrets do I already have, and what will I regret if I continue along my current path?" Taking stock of your life is necessary if you're going to prioritize your actions in a way that makes sense and is concordant with your long-term values.

Lupu and Ruiz-Castro emphasize establishing a work-life balance isn't something you do once, then don't have to worry about again. Instead, periodically reassess your life and priorities and adjust when you notice you're suffering because of work-life imbalance. However, if you can find even one area of your life to find some balance, such as asking your boss if you can leave one hour early on Fridays so you can catch your child's soccer ball, it may help your well-being.

Once you determine what you need, you can work toward finding a way to get what you need, if applicable. That's why Pattem emphasized the importance of asking for what you need from your boss. "Be honest with your boss. Do you need time off?" Or, if you're an employee who works from home but needs to get out of the house, ask for on-site work. Pattem stated each of us is different and needs to figure out what is best for them at the time. If an employee doesn't know what is best for them, a good manager should be able to develop different approaches to see what works best. As Pattem said, "A good boss will ask: What do you need right now? They will help create a personalized solution for [each] individual." However, some people can't take time off, even if they need to, because they need the money. In these cases, discussing ways to deal with personal issues that carry into the workplace with your boss will be crucial.

When in situations where I am worried about something or don't know what to do, I like to use my 9–90 rule. I ask myself what the nine-year-old version of me would say about this situation and what would the ninety-year-old version of me say. For instance, will this situation even matter when I'm wise, old, and on my death bed? What would the young, care-free version of myself think? You can apply this to any worries you may have or decisions you need to make.

PARENTHOOD AND WORK STRESS

In the times of COVID-19, the boundaries between the workplace and the home have been blurred even further. Any working person has had to adapt to working from home, along with all the caveats of this new normal.

When parenthood is added to the mix, it can seem almost impossible to retain any semblance of stability, let alone any attempts at relaxation. It's the story of many and a reality for Meg McKillip Wells, a native western New Yorker who I interviewed for this book. Wells is a project coordinator for cancer clinical trials while working on a second master's degree, and she's a mother of two young children. I asked her how she's balancing it all, and she said, "Being a working mom is a learning curve!" Wells recounted how when her youngest was an infant and sleeping for very short stretches, she was sleep-deprived while also having to develop many pieces for a study at work.

It would have been very easy for Wells to let her tiredness affect her performance, but she was aware of the issue and took action before her work was affected. She said in situations like this when you can't change what's happening in your personal life, utilizing a support network can be extremely valuable. Wells was able to lean on her husband, who was also working from home and with whom she divided childcare duties. She also asked her colleagues at work for help, and they were understanding. With their help, Wells was able to pull through. She had two recommendations for other working moms facing the stress of juggling: asking for help and giving oneself grace.

One more thing from Well's story stood out to me: even while being entirely busy, she didn't forget to take care of herself. She made time to unwind through reading and music. Wells emphasized while children are priority for parents, taking care of one's own mental health is important and will serve to make one a better parent. Parents love their children, but she told me working parents should "remember *you* matter, and you should love yourself, too."

I personally have struggled to balance writing this book and being at home with my toddler and infant. I truly commend those who have learned to manage working at home, taking care of their kids, taking care of their house, and home-schooling. Mothers (including other caretakers) are expected to work at full capacity while also performing their duties as parents at full capacity.

To help myself, I decided to hire a babysitter for four hours in the morning to focus on my book. However, my son frequently just wants me and runs into the office saying, "Mama, Mama!" I feel a lot of mom guilt when I take time away from my son to do other tasks for myself. I know that is common for many caretakers. I feel I should be spending time with my son, as this time is fleeting. It feels like a no-win situation; I feel guilty for working and feel guilty for not working, which fuels feelings of overwhelm, exhaustion, and defeat, leading to burnout.

What's worse is being judged by others for whatever decision you make. As a stay-at-home mom, I received comments like, "What do you do all day?" or, "Don't you want to do other things with your life? What about your career?" Working moms often receive comments like, "I would never put my child in daycare at the age of six months," or, "Don't you feel sad you miss a lot of your child's first moments?" Whatever comments you may receive, it's important to remember you are the best parent for your child, and you will always do what's in their best interest. First and foremost, you must take care of yourself and your family, and if that means putting your child in daycare, so be it, and if that means being a stay-at-home mom, then so be it. It's your life, your decision, and people will always have their own opinions, so let them be.

However, I remind myself before I was a mother, I was Massoma, my own individual person. I also have needs, wants, and dreams to fulfill. If I take care of myself and follow my passion, I will ultimately be a better mother and role model for my son. I find I am more patient and present with my kids when I take time to take care of myself and my mental health.

As Sheryl G. Zeigler, author and mother, emphasizes in *Harvard Business Review*, these problems have gotten even more difficult during the pandemic. Getting childcare has become even more complicated, and at the same time, working parents and especially mothers have had to work from home. She writes, "As a result, guilt is permeating everywhere as kids spend more time on screens and moms spend more time on Zoom." Once you add the emotions of guilt to an already stressful situation, it becomes even harder to navigate the stress and keep it from affecting your work.

The solution, according to Zeigler, is to acknowledge and let go of these guilty feelings.

She offers five suggestions for how you can do this:

- First, acknowledge your feelings of guilt and work on forgiving yourself. Reframe your thoughts in this manner: "Every time you think to yourself, 'I feel bad about ____,' replace that with, 'I made that decision because ____,' and move forward."
- Second, revisit your values; if your top priority as a parent is spending time with your family, spend more time with your family rather than spending time on other parenting-related activities like volunteering for the school board.
- Third, ask for help. Wells and I already emphasized the vital role of support networks but remember you need to ask for help to receive it.
- Fourth, stop trying to be perfect and be okay with being a "good enough" parent. Zeigler suggests to, "Lower the bar from the perfect mom who can do it all, who does everything she 'should' be doing and is praised for her selflessness to the mother who reclaims her own life and takes care of herself. Rather than putting additional pressure on yourself, remember the basics."
- Finally, if you follow accounts on social media that make you feel like you're not a good enough parent, unfollow them.

It hasn't been easy finishing up my book while being pregnant twice then having both my kids, but being able to separate my guilt from each individual stressor and then dealing with it has been very helpful. I've had to struggle with extreme physical fatigue, pregnancy brain (yes, it's a real thing!), and the mental fatigue that comes from being a mother. However, I hope one day when my kids see their mama wrote a book that helped many people with their anxiety and stress, they will feel proud. This one is for them.

WHEN IT'S NOT YOU, IT'S THE WORK

When I first met Sobia Mirza in 2018, we were at an outdoor get together in a mutual friend's backyard on a sunny, beautiful July afternoon. I was intrigued by her knowledge and passion about eating healthy and plant-based nutrition. I was sure she was a nutritionist or some derivative of that field, but to my surprise, she turned out to be a radiologist. She shared that she went into radiology and medical school because of her parents' influence to pursue a technical career that would give her job stability, not because she was passionate about the field. While Mirza did end up in a very secure field, she had to battle through many mental health lapses, so I contacted her and asked if I could interview her for this book.

During medical school, she suffered from physical symptoms such as heart palpitations and a tight chest. She also suffered mentally, with a feeling of dread following her as she went to classes, work, and the hospital. Her anxiety and depression were so intense they affected her socially. She had trouble getting along with classmates; she felt judged and bullied and didn't feel like she fit in. These feelings could have been caused by the competitive nature of medical school, but they were also largely because of Mirza's anxiety and depression. She had built up anger inside, and this led to her lashing out at people and making harsh comments toward others. At the time, it was hard for Mirza to recognize her aggressive behavior because, from her point of view, everyone was after her and she needed to be defensive.

Mirza had to put in an insane amount of work to succeed in residency, partially due to the sheer difficulty of residency, but also because she was not fully engaged or excited about the work. She stated, "At the end of the day, I wasn't coming home and saying, 'Well, it's worth it because I'm so excited about what I'm doing.'" Instead, she was telling herself she just had to get through it.

With her anxiety and depression struggles worsening, she went to therapy. Mirza's therapist discovered she had a lot of anger in her. She was angry about many things— from the injustices of the residency life to her not being listened to at work about the inefficiencies of the hospital system. She was also angry about how she was treated as a radiologist in the hospital. In her words, she was treated like a lab tech and felt like she had lost all control of her position. People were always pulling her in different directions, calling her, and demanding she do things, and the pressures started to get to her. She had to learn how to tell others no and what to do when she was feeling behind, and she had to figure out how to prevent others from walking over her and what to do when she wasn't in control of her workflow.

Mirza's unhappiness and anxiety were also caused by the healthcare system in general. She quickly saw she did not agree with some parts of the healthcare field. Things she considered important were not necessarily considered important in the healthcare field, and leadership within the hospital did not seem to be on her side. She observed blatant racism, sexism, and more. Ultimately, this disgusted her.

Then she shifted her studies to a pediatric fellowship, and things started to look up. The people were nicer, the systems more organized, her work life was less demanding and hectic. "We were a more critical part of the team and our opinions mattered," she said. People genuinely wanted to know what she thought, and she had enthusiastic teachers who were excited to work with her one on one. Additionally, she found out her personality meshed better with the personalities of people working in pediatrics. Within this fellowship, she also became aware of the joy she felt by being able to physically see the patient and the result of her work.

Finally, she got a job as a pediatric radiologist at Children's National Hospital in Washington, DC. She was an attending physician, but she soon found herself experiencing the same upsetting workplace issues that had angered her as a resident. This was when Mirza decided to start looking into lifestyle medicine. She started reading up on it, going to conferences, and talking to people about the opportunities that are out there for her. When she started talking to other people about their experiences with lifestyle medicine, she realized she wanted to—and could—pursue it as a career. She decided to study obesity medicine and cut down on her full-time hours as a radiologist.

At this point, Mirza was also back in therapy because she had started to have anxiety about going to work. This was accompanied by symptoms: trouble sleeping, waking up with palpitations, and chest tightness. She would dread going to work all night and wake up with intense anxiety. Once Mirza actually got to work, she would feel fine, but she noticed herself becoming angry again and resentful toward others. This was when Mirza realized something had to change.

She decided to try and help herself fit better into her workplace by reading self-help books. Mirza aimed to make herself more efficient and productive at work, hoping this would make her enjoy her job more. Over time, she concluded she was not the problem. It was the job. So, she gave a PowerPoint presentation detailing all the inefficiencies at work and offering solutions as to how to fix them. Other radiologists at the hospital supported her PowerPoint and her stance, agreeing they felt similar stress on the job. However, after her presentation, she found out her workplace did not have the time or resources to take care of these inefficiencies. That was it. She finally decided not to put any more effort into fixing the workplace. Since she was unable to change the workplace, she would make a change in her life and get out of it.

Mirza finally told the hospital she was quitting to make a plant-based weight loss program for children. Although she was still working for the hospital part-time due to the pandemic, she found the time to open her own clinic from home. Mirza was slowly starting to see patients and building up the reputation of her clinic. She shared her dream was to run the clinic for twenty hours per week and to work as a radiologist from home. Finally, for Mirza, there was a light at the end of the tunnel, and amazingly, her anger had lifted. It became easier for her to find patience and compassion for others because she was doing what she loves.

Mirza also began to practice mindfulness and meditation to minimize her anxiety. She has slowly learned to apply these mindfulness practices to her daily life, allowing herself to take control of her mind. As she explained, "When I am stressed, I'm able to take a moment, pause, and remind myself to breathe." Now, in the mornings, she and her husband practice a mindfulness routine that includes journaling and meditation.

Overall, one message Mirza emphasizes and wants to spread to people is, "Feeling something hasn't worked out or something is not a good fit is different than thinking you're a failure." She highlighted that you have not failed by not being the right fit. You just need to go out and find something that fits better. Mirza's path to finding a career that made her happy had many bumps in the road, but Mirza took control of what she could: her mental health. Throughout medical school, her residency, and her fellowship, whenever she struggled with her mental health, she went to therapy and used the techniques learned there to get through it. Now, after getting through all of that, she has finally found her dream job and has surrounded her life with mindfulness practices such as meditation, journaling, and exercising. Mirza is a shining example showing we can take back power in our lives when we learn to listen to and respect ourselves by taking care of not only our physical health but also our mental health.

CONCLUSION

Finding your work-life balance is about looking at what issues are causing a lack of balance and then asking for what you need so you have a more ideal lifestyle. For some, this work includes resolving past issues that are affecting your emotions and actions at work. In the case of mothers, getting out from under the shadow of guilt and judgment is important so you can make the best decisions for yourself and your family. As Mirza shows us, sometimes the answer to work stress isn't to shift the balance. Those strong feelings against your workplace might just be indicating there's a different opportunity out there that will be more aligned with your purpose and what you care most about. In the next chapter, I look at the role mental and physical clutter can have in your workplace stress and what you can do to decrease stress through minimalism.

CHAPTER SEVEN

MINIMIZE THE CLUTTER

As I mentioned in the last chapter, even hearing a beeping sound would cause me to start feeling anxious at work, as the sound reminded me of the hospital machines. It took me years to process what had happened. I would experience moments of depersonalization, which is feeling like you are observing yourself from outside your body, and it is the sense life around you is not real. I would call it "weird feelings" because I had no idea what was happening. I kept it to myself for years and just pushed through. I thought I was going crazy, but it was easier to ignore these sensations than to face them.

Over time, not dealing with my trauma led to panic attacks and even agoraphobia (fear of being trapped in unsafe environments). Halfway through medical school, I had to drop out because the anxiety consumed me. It was too mentally taxing. I could not sleep, wasn't eating well, and had lost weight. I was living in a constant state of fear. Can you imagine continually being afraid? That was my life. I had moments where I didn't want to live anymore. The pain was so intense.

The painful memories I was carrying were a form of mental clutter. They were items that once served a purpose to keep me safe when I was hospitalized and scared, but which no longer served me as a healthy adult. It can feel overwhelming to begin noticing how events in your childhood and the past can influence present day stressors in your life but doing so can be life changing. With awareness of your mental clutter, you can choose not to give it power any longer, which you will see in my example from leadership trainer and author Jake Melton. With minimalism, he declutters both mental and physical stressors.

Physical clutter can also create anxiety and stress that affect your work and sense of well-being, as you may have gathered from the popular *Tidying Up With Marie Kondo* Netflix series. Often, multitasking goes hand in hand with physical and mental clutter and the resulting lack of focus and stress, which was certainly the case for me. When you do the work of uncluttering your mind and apply the same discipline to your workspace and schedule, even more potential opens for stress and anxiety to reduce so something new can emerge—maybe even joy.

THE PRINCIPLE OF MINIMALISM

"When I was diagnosed with Tourette syndrome, I felt something was really wrong with me and worried nobody would want to be my friend," said Jake Melton, a mindset coach, productivity and simplicity expert, and the author of *Minimize to Maximize Your Happiness: Cut the Crap.* I interviewed him because his book made a big impact on my understanding of how my hospitalization affected me so profoundly later in life. Melton could totally relate.

He shared that when he was fourteen years old, after being diagnosed with Tourette syndrome, his father was diagnosed with a fatal illness. As the eldest of five children, Melton had to step up and take care of the family and spent a lot of time in the hospital visiting with his father. This led to a further decline in Melton's mental health; he was ultimately diagnosed with depression and anxiety. After college, his father passed away, and the son fell deeper into depression and anxiety. In addition to the Tourette syndrome diagnosis, he has also suffered from obsessive-compulsive disorder (OCD) and attention deficit disorder (ADD). He was even diagnosed with PTSD at one point. With all these issues, he doubted he would never get married or fulfill his dream of becoming a public speaker.

Then he discovered minimalism. The philosophy behind minimalism includes essentialism, simplicity, saving time, and abiding by the principle that everything has a purpose and intention with nothing extra. These values and the activities he started to support minimalism resulted in positive improvements in Melton's quality of life and his mental health. As he said, "I took up the minimalist journey to help me live a more focused, productive, and purposeful life." Eventually, the minimalist lifestyle helped Melton deal with his stress and anxiety as he eliminated his mental clutter. "There was mental and emotional healing a minimalist lifestyle could bring me," he told me. "Medicine and therapy weren't working for me in dealing with my mental health battles, but minimalism . . . helped me eliminate risks of added anxiety, lower levels of depression, and start living a happier, simpler, more productive lifestyle." As the mental clutter lifted, something else shifted for him.

In his book, Melton describes how to attain more purpose, success, and time in your life by getting rid of toxic relationships, mental clutter, and things that keep you from finding peace and joy in your life. Minimalism isn't an overnight decision; it is a journey that takes time to achieve. Cutting the crap is a positive movement that empowers you to get rid of the negative and embrace the positive in your life, home, business, workplace, and own mind. Whether you are looking to find peace in a demanding world or you are attempting to grow a business, these ideas and principles will help you achieve added happiness and clarity in your life.

Melton's use of minimalism spilled over from his personal life to his professional one. He described how he helps organizations and entrepreneurs as "streamlining . . . [to] gain improved profits by minimizing basic things like bills, subscriptions, processes, paper supply." As his clients minimize their tasks, they can instead focus resources on strategies that would "increase their happiness and that of their employees as well." Here, decluttering physical items and processes increased happiness in the workplace.

In a specific example, he told me a customer story about an organization with a high turnover rate. He diagnosed the issue and discovered employees felt they were wasting their time in meetings because those meetings didn't help them make sales (employees at this firm were compensated by commission). He brought this finding to the company's executives and asked if they could reduce the frequency of the meeting times or utilize alternative methods of communication, such as email. The company's executives agreed. After following Melton's advice, they noted the turnover rate had decreased. They also shared the company's employees now felt their time was being better valued and their roles were now adequately aligned with their personal goals and mission. Melton laughed, "The leaders just had to cut the crap!" In other words, they decluttered both with less meetings and less frustration.

His approach makes me think of Sobia Mirzas' story from Chapter Six. She tried to suggest workplace changes that would have prevented inefficiencies and increased joy, but they weren't implemented, and she left. She removed that toxic work from her life, a move Melton has made himself. Once he had a coworker who stressed him out to a point Melton began to eat lunch with a different group of people. "I removed myself from that situation, and that helped," Melton says. In this case, he decluttered his lunch break. In a more extreme example, once he also left a job because he felt the business had unethical practices. That was extreme decluttering and an example of this maxim he follows: "Don't waste your time on things that will not help you grow or improve. Practice time management and streamlining workplace processes." If we declutter things that aren't helpful, we make room for more good things.

When discussing the importance of reducing your mental workload to help decrease stress, Melton noted, "The fewer things going on in your life, the less there is to worry about and . . . remember." This is especially poignant when I think about my own stress when I was hospitalized. Of course, my anxiety was incredibly high because I was going through so much, but that doesn't have to be the rest of my life's story.

Today, Melton is the father of two children, a beautiful girl and a boy. He has also taken the stage on many occasions, speaking to large audiences with thousands of people. He did not let his disease stop him. He said, "Nothing can stop us if we don't allow it to." Here's a final suggestion from Melton on the art of minimizing stress: "Think about who and what is trying to make you a better person." For anything or anyone in your life not making you a better person, Melton said, "Cut it out. . . . First, clear your physical clutter; make it light, clean, and open. Then, declutter your mind through meditation and mindfulness." Ah, that sounds refreshing.

JOY AT WORK

When you first read the phrase, "joy at work," what comes to your mind? For many readers, I imagine this might sound like a strange joke. Work can be so stressful and anxiety-filled, and to get from there to feeling joy is a huge leap. It's also a possible one. In *Joy at Work* by organizational guru Marie Kondo and business professor Scott Sonenshein, they share a variety of solutions to reduce of one of the largest contributors to stress and anxiety and work: clutter. Kondo employs a strategy that is rooted in the philosophy that an individual should only keep possessions which "spark joy." Kondo's strategies can be applied to the maintenance of both a tidier physical and digital workplace. Sure, it takes a lot of energy to clean and maintain your workplace, but in return, you get the ability to use your time more efficiently.

Before I dealt with my past trauma, I had the mental clutter of that stress, and it also spilled into my workspace and performance. I found myself trying to multitask, which meant I always had many screens and files open for different projects at any given time, and my desk was piled with different files and papers. It wasn't clear what was urgent or what my system was for finding what I needed—in fact, I barely had one. Like many busy people, I felt all those tasks and paperwork were a badge of honor for how hard I was working. In fact, I was disorganized mentally and also in my physical and digital space. Maybe some of you can relate, and a decluttering might be in order.

At the heart of Kondo's organizational method is a simple evaluation process you can apply to decluttering any aspect of your workplace, including physical and digital office space. The most important elements of Kondo's organization method on work clutter include:

- How to get started: The best way to help declutter your digital life is to start by organizing your computer's desktop and email inbox.

- What to do: To create a tidier workspace, examine your current collection of books and papers and decide whether or not they are useful or spark joy.
- Why this matters: An organized workspace will help you become more productive, profitable, and happy, which will in turn cause your boss to have a higher opinion of you.

Essentially, Kondo's organizational process begins with a general assessment of your current belongings. You then evaluate each item and assign it to one of three joy-themed categories: immediate joy, functional joy, or future joy. If you discover items in your workspace that don't elicit one of these feelings, then get rid of them. It's that simple.

Kondo advises you create an end goal for your decluttering and ask yourself what you'd like to see in your joyful workspace. I find this is the hardest part of her process, but it's worth doing, so play along. Envision how that would make you feel. Notice what's in this space and be specific. Envision how you see each item placed in this workspace and the emotions you experience while you're in this space. This will likely be the most difficult task to accomplish because it requires a great deal of visualization. This step is the most critical and will determine how likely it is you will maintain the changes you execute.

Now that you've completed the hardest step, you're ready to begin the work. I organized my digital clutter by looking at what I actually needed to focus on right then and moved everything else to an external hard drive. This allowed me to quickly find what I needed to access day to day. Then for information I might need to refer to or old projects I might want to review again, I could find them when I needed them, but I didn't have to scroll through them every time I needed a file.

Next, examine your email management. The key here is to treat your email inbox as if it's a place to house current projects, not as a means for permanent storage. While this may seem obvious, this simple change will result in a significant reduction in the amount of your work stress. Consider how much time you spend searching for emails or how overwhelmed you feel when you open your email and it's completely full. If it's too difficult to sort through all the emails now, then throw all the existing emails into an archive folder to organize at a later date. I caution you not to let this task sit uncompleted. This is a crucial step to help organize your workspace and increase your happiness at work.

My personal favorite digital decluttering advice is to set office hours for responding to emails. I turn on "do not disturb" on my cell phone from seven o'clock in the morning to noon every day so I can work without being distracted by new emails. Since incorporating my office hours, I've noticed a significant boost to my productivity, and I manage my workplace stress more easily.

With your digital space organized, let's look at your physical workspace. Collect all the books in your workspace and place them in front of you. As Kondo advises, pick each of them up and ask yourself, "Does this spark joy?" A way to help you answer this question is to identify whether you feel happier knowing this item is actually in your workspace. This will also help you determine the best way to organize your space, because you may discover while the item brings you joy, its position in your physical workspace is not contributing to your joy. Grab a trash can and eliminate the stuff you don't need and increase your happiness.

Sometimes you can't just throw things away at work, right? Someone is going to ask to see a report that doesn't give you joy. I agree with Kondo that paperwork is a little different and maybe can't all be thrown away, but you can still sort it by category and get it off your desk and into a file system that makes sense so you can find what you need when you need it, and things that aren't a high priority are out of sight. No more fishing through a messy desk drawer that has a mix of all these file types, but also has downright trash.

As you might imagine, decluttering can make you better at your job. All the time you spend looking for things is time you're not making progress on your projects and deadlines. A survey done by OfficeMax in 2011 published in *PR Newswire* showed:

- Ninety percent of Americans identified clutter as a source of diminished happiness, productivity, and motivation.
- Seven percent of respondents to that survey said clutter harms their productivity; half of respondents said a lack of organization worsens their state of mind and decreases motivation.

- Around 40 percent said clutter harms their professional image ("An Unorganized Nation," 2011).

If you can learn to maintain a clean workspace, you're going to be happier, more productive, and more profitable.

If that's not enough to convince you to de-clutter, consider all of the hours of lost productivity which result from the collective time spent searching for important documents or supplies. In fact, this is a strategy Melton used for one of his clients in the previous section of this chapter, and that company reported happier and more productive employees. I know decluttering is going to be a difficult task for a lot of you because we have been raised to consider this wasteful. Consider how much of your time has already been wasted as a result of the presence of this item in the larger sea of clutter in your office. Remember the goal is to reduce clutter, which will in turn result in an increase in your efficiency, productivity, and, most importantly, your overall happiness.

I most love that Marie Kondo's method doesn't focus on organization for the sake of cleanliness. It serves a functional purpose that is intended to increase the level of joy in an individual's life. Speaking for myself, I can attest to the fact that when my workspace is neat and positioned in an intentional manner and is in a location that helps me work more efficiently, my work life is significantly improved. There is a direct relationship between the physical state of your work environment and the emotional state of your work life.

CLEAR MULTITASKING FROM YOUR SCHEDULE

When working at the nonprofit, in a single morning I'd want to accomplish my lesson plans, do research for a grant, design a flyer, organize a gala, and create strategic partnerships at the same time as a super-employee. There would be a lot of tabs open on my computer, and I'd have a lot of fleeting thoughts in my mind. An hour could go by, and I would have nothing to show for it but incomplete tasks. I would think of things to do and decide to do them later, but not write those thoughts down, so I would forget. Multitasking wasn't productive at all for me. Instead, it created clutter on my desk, desktop, email account, and even in the back seat of my car.

I brought up multitasking with Bonnie St. John, the best-selling author and resilience expert we met in Chapter Five, when I interviewed her. It turns out multitasking is antithetical to her micro-resilience strategy. Instead, she said, "Multitasking is a source of exhaustion; you can reduce it by creating zones of focus. Focus for one hour, then take a break, and you will be more productive." That's very similar to what I did when I started taking note of my to-dos so I could finish a single task at a time. St. John continued, "Multitasking is fine as long as you don't need quality and innovation, but if you want quality work, you need to focus on one task at a time." She's right. Another change I made was to do the easiest tasks first to check them off—those that didn't need quality or innovation, so then I'd have more time and creative focus to do the more specific tasks and big projects.

In her book *Micro-Resilience: Minor Shifts for Major Boosts in Focus, Drive, and Energy*, St. John mentions scientists like Daniel Kahneman, author of *Attention and Effort*, have done a lot of research which proves multitasking is not effective. He states:

"Proficiency disintegrates rapidly when we try to multitask our way through a normal workday. Performing multiple activities that involve complexities like decision making and analysis slows us down even more dramatically. When our thought process is divided, our ability to recall details diminishes. We significantly reduce impulses for creativity, and we increase the risk of serious mistakes—all of which contribute to an overall reduction in the quality of our work" (St. John 2017).

As he points out, competing tasks, meetings, and projects can create serious clutter in our minds and make us less effective. It's possible if you feel stressed about your work, the issue just might be trying to juggle too many things without a strategy in place to manage them.

The company eBay has a solution to decrease distractions for employees. In my interview with her, St. John shared, "They have a conference room for one, where on the wall you will see a big sign that says 'FOCUS.' This is where employees can focus and get their work done in a quiet space." Even if you can't find a quiet place in your work environment, you might be able to silence some apps or notifications and turn your phone on silent to be more productive. "It's difficult to focus nowadays with our phones and technology always pulling our attention one way or the other," St. John said. Indeed, and all of those distractions and the inability to focus increase our stress.

There are many ways in which multitasking increases stress and splits our attention so we try to do too much at once and accomplish little. As Laurie Cameron, author of *The Mindful Day: Practical Ways to Find Focus, Calm and Joy from Morning to Evening*, puts it, "Multitasking keeps us out of the present moment, and that's where we feel more space and ease." To get back into the present when you get into the mind clutter of multitasking, begin to notice when it's happening and refocus to be less stressed and more productive.

Cameron suggests you can start your whole day with a clear focus for your schedule: "In the morning, choose a single project to focus on and set a goal that's timebound. For instance, you'll work on it for sixty minutes, then take a break." This echoes St. John's advice to take breaks every hour to increase focus. There are many ways to take short breaks, such as, "Go for a walk outside or draw or close your eyes and focus on your breath—something that gives your prefrontal cortex, the reasoning and thinking part of your brain, a break" (Cameron, 2018).

CONCLUSION

Sometimes, as for Melton and myself, you might have past traumas which aren't healed and are creating mental clutter. In other situations, your clutter could be digital files or applications that are obsolete or distracting. You might have physical clutter in your workspace making it tough to find what you need because so many things around you aren't necessary. The same method will help you clear all these types of clutter. Practice minimalism and get rid of anything not essential to your happiness and desired outcomes. Or, as Kondo puts it, throw out what doesn't spark joy for you. Decide where it's best for you to start this process, choose something to let go of, and discard it. Ah, doesn't that feel better? Apply the same process to tasks you do throughout your day to increase your focus and reduce stress by kicking multitasking to the curb. In the next chapter, I share more about decreasing work stress by changing the way you look at common work stressors like deadlines, procrastination, and performance anxiety.

CHAPTER EIGHT

HOW TO GET THE JOB DONE

After my TEDx pitch was accepted, everything was supposed to be easier. For months, I had researched my topic and strategized my talk. Now, I was on the speaker list for TEDx Wilmington, and all I had to do was practice and be ready for the big day.

What could go wrong?

As the weeks passed, I would do anything instead of practicing my talk. This was nothing new because I'm a big procrastinator and would often leave my tasks for the last minute. Years ago, while I was doing my master's degree, I would submit my assignments at 11:59 p.m. for a midnight deadline. I know, I still shake my head when I think about it. I would put off tasks because the thought of them and the amount of work I needed to do would overwhelm me, so I would just avoid them. Also, I avoided my work because I put high expectations on myself! I would do other simpler tasks and just put off the more complex assignments until the very last minute. I'd then feel guilt or regret. It was a cycle I was stuck in.

Years later while working on the TEDx Talk, I still hadn't broken it. Every time I thought about giving my talk, I would imagine the mistakes I would probably make. It felt safer not to practice than to do so and mess up. Sometimes I felt if I couldn't complete a task perfectly, then I wouldn't do it at all. Perfectionism and procrastination tend to be connected, in that perfectionism breeds procrastination, leading to nothing being accomplished. "Perfectionism is almost always fear-based and a symptom of some type of mental disorder, it's never considered 'healthy,' even in everyday people," clinical psychologist Dr. Erin Grinstead told me when I interviewed her. Perfectionism is not a diagnostic term but is usually a symptom of another disorder such as anxiety, depression, or obsessive-compulsive personality disorder. This was me.

In addition to putting off practicing to later, I wondered how I would perform the talk without having a panic attack. The very thought of being on stage in front of a crowd of accomplished professionals made my hands break out in a sweat, and my pulse would quicken. This performance anxiety also fed into the procrastination cycle because I would avoid practicing to prevent my anxiety from flaring up. Something had to change as the date of the event was approaching.

Then, I took my own advice. The subject of my talk was the D.A.R.E. four-step system, founded by author and anxiety coach Barry McDonagh. He offers a comprehensive suite of tools, including a Facebook support group, an app, calls with a therapist, group calls, bootcamps, audio training, Instagram videos, and more. These resources helped me overcome my anxiety, as well as get to the bottom of my perfectionism and better my procrastination.

In this chapter, you will meet McDonagh and learn about his methods. I also share the best tips that helped me practice and be on the TEDx stage to give a performance I'm proud of. I also examine the causes of procrastination and what's going on when we dread a deadline. You'll also learn how to work with your brain to hit your deadlines without procrastinating—at least not *much*.

D.A.R.E. YOUR PERFORMANCE ANXIETY

Given how valuable I found Barry McDonagh's help when I was preparing for my TEDx Talk, I invited him to speak with me about overcoming performance anxiety for this book. He is the creator of the bestselling anxiety treatment program Panic Away, and author of *DARE: A New Way to End Anxiety and Stop Panic Attacks*. The four steps of his system to decrease anxiety include:

- Defuse the situation and turn "what if this or that?" to "so what?"
- Allow yourself to feel the anxiety instead of trying to stop it
- Run toward the triggering activity by telling yourself you're excited and looking forward to the performance
- Engage your mind with an activity so your body can relax

When you apply these principles together, you'll start feeling better when performing the activity and sometimes permanently shift the anxiety altogether.

In our conversation, he shared that performance anxiety is especially prominent in workers who do public services, such as hairdressers, videographers, dental hygienists, or doctors. One symptom of performance anxiety they often experience is hand trembling. When this happens, he said, "They are afraid the public will see them acting anxiously and, because they're meant to be professional, that doesn't come across well." So, their careers depend on addressing this anxiety to get rid of the shaky hands symptom. I found when I have shaky hands, taking slow, deep belly breaths and imagining breathing into my hands (or whatever problematic area) and taking nice slow exhales really helps.

McDonagh advises these workers to *defuse* the situation if it's appropriate and let the client know, "my hands get a little shaky sometimes." This helps because their worst fear is the client will see the shaky hands and judge them. Another tip is to *allow* the physical manifestations of anxiety to happen and not to try to stop or block the feelings. Doing so enables the anxiety to run its course. Then, *run toward* the issue by reminding yourself you love cutting hair, which attaches a new meaning to the anxiety to make it positive instead of negative. Run toward could even entail saying, "Okay hands, shake even more, flail your hands all over the place, go ahead!" This may make you chuckle a bit, which in return deescalates the intensity of the anxious moment. Lastly, *engage* in an activity like tidying your workstation, which gives your mind another focus so your body can release the anxiety.

He said *defuse* is often the hardest part of his system for people to follow. Many people don't like to share their anxiety because they think it's unprofessional. He's found those who do so may relieve a lot of the anxiety, and their relationship with their client may also get stronger because of their openness and honesty. For my speech, just knowing I could say, "I'm a little nervous to give this speech," helped me feel less nervous.

When people see each other as humans and not just someone with whom they are transacting, the interpersonal dynamic changes. Imagine what it's like to be anxious and trying to hide it, and when you fear others are noticing your face is blushing, you feel even more nervous. Anxiety or embarrassment are not as obvious to others as we often imagine. "So, in our own heads, we think everyone can see exactly what's happening and how terrified we are. But we can be very good at hiding these manifestations," said McDonagh. When you share what's going on instead of trying to cover it up, the anxiety can dissipate or even lift entirely. This is especially true for the workplace.

After I did my TEDx Talk, numerous people approached me and asked how I had the courage to be so vulnerable on stage in front of a hundred people and how I managed to memorize my whole ten-minute speech. Here are some of my tips:

- Defuse: Imagine a funny situation, such as your audience is farting. Something about farts is just so funny, and if you can see your audience as funny, it's more difficult to see them as terrifying or as a source of danger.
- Allow: Take a few deep breaths to relax and let your nerves work themselves out.
- Run toward: One trick I use for public speaking when I am feeling nervous is telling myself, "I am excited by this feeling!" Turn your nervousness into excitement and energy. You can trick your brain by repeatedly saying, "I'm excited!" Because both nervousness and excitement are emotions of an adrenaline rush, it's just our mind's perception that is the lens of our outlook. Change your lens to change your outlook.
- Engage: Before getting up to the stage, pump yourself up by playing a motivational song such as "Ain't No Mountain High Enough" by Marvin Gaye and Tammi Terrell or "The Nights" by Avicii.

Another strategy that uses multiple D.A.R.E. principles at once is to defuse the tension by focusing on one or two of the audience members and imagining you are having a conversation with them, which engages your mind. It's hard to speak to a crowd, but you already know how to have a conversation with one or two other people, so now you can run toward the stage. Once you start, it's smooth sailing.

If all else fails, "go spaghetti," as I say in my TEDx Talk, and learn to laugh at yourself. Now, don't drown your feelings in a bowl of pasta—unless you want to. What

I mean is to go spaghetti and let your muscles relax, go limp. Unclench your jaw, drop your shoulders, relax your forehead, soften your shoulders, and let the anxiety run through you. In this way, you release yourself from the emotions by letting them run their course.

UNDERSTAND DEADLINES AND PROCRASTINATION

Whereas performance anxiety occurs when you have to do an activity in public, procrastination is a major cause of stress for many people that's most often private, especially when a deadline is looming. We feel as if we are racing against the clock, especially if we leave tasks until the last minute. Procrastination can even cause people to resent their tasks, when in reality they may hate that the task has to be done in a rush. Also, procrastination can cause a lot of guilt, self-doubt, and make you feel like you are "lazy" or not a hard worker. Charlotte Liberman explains in her 2019 *New York Times* article, "Self-awareness is a key part of why procrastinating makes us feel so rotten." When we procrastinate, we are fully aware it's a bad idea, and we are deliberately avoiding the task at hand anyway.

Procrastination can become a cycle of guilt. You feel you're behind on your work and thoughts such as, "What's wrong with me, why can't I just finish my work on time?" start to pop in, and then the stress of "What will happen if I miss the deadline?" increases. I suffered from this vicious cycle in graduate school. Basic behaviorism shows being rewarded prompts us to continue the actions that reaped those rewards, so as I would procrastinate, my brain would reward me with a temporary high. That's how procrastination can quickly turn into routine, falling into a cycle that is hard to break according to Jane Kinney in a 2021 article for *Zenerations*. According to Kinney, there are a number of ways to break out of this cycle of procrastination, including:

- Be aware you are procrastinating.
- Understand why you're procrastinating.
- Have an accountability buddy, someone who can check on your progress.
- Verbally commit yourself to the task you need to do; you may even write it on paper.
- Reward yourself and celebrate when you don't procrastinate and get the task done!
- Remember as you do unwanted tasks, you'll have more time for more enjoyable things.

As she explains, it's important to understand you are procrastinating and why, then to solve the issues at the root of your procrastination. Procrastination is a difficult habit to kick, but like any other habit or repeated behavior, you have the power to change it.

I used her framework to stop putting off my speech practice. I had to be honest with myself that nothing else was going on except I was avoiding the work. This opened space for me to consider the root of why I was procrastinating. Through the D.A.R.E response book, I did find a community and even a therapist to keep me accountable to my practice times. I did write on my calendar when I was committing the time to practice. The biggest anti-procrastination habit I formed was rewarding myself afterward and playing with my son. It pained me to shut the door and practice (which made me procrastinate), but afterward it was so much fun to see what games he wanted to play and feel guilt-free about it.

With all this in mind, let's take another look at deadlines and how they impact procrastination. Most things you put off will have an end date, as there was a date for the TEDx event, my term papers, and even this book's completion. These deadlines can cause stress for two key reasons:

1. First, unrealistic deadlines might be impossible to meet, in which case it's a great idea to talk to your supervisor and see if your deadlines can be adjusted to something more reasonable.
2. Second, realistic and reasonable deadlines can be a source of stress if you tend to procrastinate or don't budget your time well.

When you admit you are procrastinating and seek to understand why, you'll discover which of the two problems you have and what to do about it. If the deadline is unreasonable, why? Who can help? What do you need to ask for? Then in other cases, look to solve the issues that are at the root of your procrastination if the deadline is realistic. Are you not managing your time well? What anxiety could be stopping you? What busy work are you putting in the way? To avoid this task, what are you doing instead, and is there a cycle you can break? The answers will help you understand and solve the issue.

Finally, the disappointment we fear we may feel in the future or cause to others to feel if we do not meet a deadline can be a double-edged sword of a stressor. Concern that we will anger a boss or a major client, frustrate a family member, or let ourselves down can be debilitating and actually cause us to create the very disappointment we fear. Fortunately, with understanding, we can beat this stress and work with our deadlines. Here are some tips for reducing deadline stress that I find helpful:

- Make sure the deadline is reasonable, as I said earlier. Evaluate the deadline and tell your manager if you think it isn't reasonable.
- Break the deadline down into smaller subtasks and set deadlines for those. Start with the most urgent and important tasks first.
- In your calendar, do a countdown to the deadline date. For example, write "Ten days until Project X is due," "Five days until Project X is due," and so on, on the appropriate date.
- Have a contingency plan. It's always a good idea to build in some buffer space. Set your deadline a day or two earlier than the actual deadline just in case there are last-minute tweaks needed or other issues arise.
- Look at the history of past tasks being completed. Were they completed on time? Was there a delay? Use this information to plan your own timing.

These strategies should help you face your next deadline head-on and make a plan to achieve it with room to spare or communicate in advance if not so you get help and mitigate many of the worst consequences for failing to meet a deadline.

WORK WITH YOUR BRAIN

Despite working with deadlines and understanding your procrastination, what if you still aren't completing your tasks? Turns out that might not be such a bad thing according to Lithuanian psychologist Bluma Zeigarnik, who observed the effects of interruption on memory processing during the late 1920s. From this research, she coined the "Zeigarnik effect," in which our minds tend to think of things we have left unfinished. Therefore, if a task has been interrupted, we remember it more easily. In essence Jane Kinney reports in a *Psychologist World Today* blog, "The Zeigarnik Effect Explained," the Zeigarnik effect proposes people remember unfinished or interrupted tasks better than completed tasks.

Maybe working from home and having the front doorbell ring or having to take your dog out for an unscheduled break is actually making your work better. Or that coworker who knocks on your cubicle for an unscheduled chat might be doing you a favor. The benefits don't stop just with improving your memory of what's unfinished. When you're aware unfinished tasks are a constant drain on your own mental resources, you'll be motivated to complete more tasks, which will improve your memory and mental function so it's available for the most important projects.

Often understanding how your brain works is not a huge motivation to do something you're avoiding. An effective way to overcome procrastination is to just get started with an incredibly small step (Kinney, 2021). If this first step is very easy to do, it'll be easier to get started. Here's where the Zeigarnik effect is important: the essence of this effect is if a task has been started but remains unfinished, the incomplete status of the task takes up psychological energy, intruding on our thoughts. The discomfort of this leads us to continue working on the task, and only when it is done does the psychological hold loosen. This is why when you have a to-do list, physically crossing off or adding a checkmark to completed tasks feels so good. So, start somewhere and then be sure to cross off that first item.

When I was preparing for my TEDx Talk, I also procrastinated practicing because I was afraid I wouldn't be able to memorize the speech. Ever have difficulty remembering the key points in your presentation or struggle to remember how to use a new software? The struggle to easily recall new information can also lead to stress. Kinney discusses one implication of the Zeigarnik effect is that breaking down study sessions into shorter stretches can help you recall material. Cramming for long periods of time should be avoided. Instead, it's important to schedule breaks so you can focus on something else. This shift in focus leads the brain to want to remember the information you were studying, which then leads your mind to rehearse the material, establishing it more firmly (Kinney, 2021). This study method can help students better remember what was studied at exam time, and it can totally help you include all the important information when you go into a high-stakes meeting.

The roots of some mental health issues like insomnia, anxiety, and depleted mental and emotional capabilities are impacted by the Zeigarnik effect, as Kinney notes. One example is how leaving tasks unfinished creates pressure and stress as you give energy to worrying about the task, potentially leading to increased anxiety that keeps you awake at night. Then, the next day you're not well-rested and experience brain-fog from sleep deprivation. On the flip side, the Zeigarnik effect can improve your mental health (Kinney, 2021). This is because the same pressure or stress from the unfinished task can create motivation to complete it. Completing the task can then bring forth renewed self-esteem and confidence, along with feelings of accomplishment. In addition, better psychological health can be achieved from finishing particularly difficult and stressful tasks, as this can provide closure of sorts. This research is documented but not as well-known as it should be, given the beneficial implications of it.

CONCLUSION

Next time you're putting off important work or dread an activity you have to perform, try the tools in this chapter. Maybe it will help to D.A.R.E. your anxiety and work with it so you're in the driver's seat, not the anxiety. Also consider the root of what you're putting off. Is the issue the deadline itself or procrastination? Set small goals and celebrate each incremental step to make continuous progress on your projects. When all else fails, remember procrastination does have some upsides when you consider the Zeigarnik effect. Maybe leaving your task unfinished is just the thing you needed to do so a new, creative idea could appear, helping you be ready to finish strong. In the next chapter, I discuss another huge stressor around work: dealing with bosses and coworkers.

CHAPTER NINE

DEALING WITH OTHERS AT WORK

What if you have a coworker who doesn't get along with anyone? Mary (whose name has been changed to ensure anonymity) had a coworker who couldn't mix well with anyone, and she agreed to sit down with me for an interview to tell me the story. This person would go around the office complaining about other people, their work, and even how they parked their cars. It seemed there was nothing she could do when this person came to her desk except agree with her to make that coworker stop gossiping and leave her desk. They would just go find the next person to repeat the same grievances to. At first, she wondered if the concerns were legitimate, but over time she learned this person never stopped complaining about others, and she was curious about what was being said about her when she wasn't around.

The situation was especially difficult because Mary worked in an open space environment where interpersonal issues can become particularly problematic because you just can't shut a door between yourself and others.

All the gossiping created tension in the open coworking space, which made working uncomfortable. "I think in order for an open coworking space to be effective, your human resources needs to be on point," she told me. "You can't pick someone who you know won't go well with the rest of the team . . . especially if your staff is small. Balancing personalities—knowing what will work best with who, who shouldn't be near who—should all be thought out before hiring someone." However, while she waited for management to address the situation, she still had to go to work every day and do her best despite the tension.

It's not just Mary. Many of the people I interviewed experienced issues with their coworkers that added to their overall stress. As you probably know, coworkers can be a significant source of work stress. People have different personalities and different perspectives; most people carry some emotional baggage with them that can affect the way they perceive and respond to work situations. Even during the COVID-19 pandemic, when many people have been working from home, there can be tense Zoom meetings and increased miscommunications as more conversations happen by email and text instead of in-person. We have to navigate all of this while doing our jobs, which have their own built-in stressors.

Mary's suggestion to deal with negative coworkers, when quitting isn't an option, is "removing yourself from that work environment when it gets too intense and doing your work elsewhere (if your boss allows for it). I would go to coffee shops to do my work if the workplace felt too toxic for me." The non-confrontational approach can work at times because we can't control people in the office or otherwise, but we can control our reactions to them. It is not realistic to think everyone will like us and we will always like everyone. However, in a professional setting, it is important to try and be cordial with our coworkers.

Each person I spoke to about the topic of stressful coworkers and bosses had different suggestions for how to deal with interpersonal stressors at work. These strategies are different depending on your relationship with the coworker who is causing stress. Or are they a person you have to deal with every day as a peer? Maybe you can come to an understanding or have a fruitful conversation with them. Are they your boss? There are still ways you can ask for what you need and seek help to resolve the issue.

MAYBE IT'S ME, NOT THEM

Jess Ruggieri, the management expert you met in Chapter Five, has a unique strategy for dealing with difficult interpersonal relationships at work. She suggests changing the way you think about your coworkers who bug you. I asked her about this approach in our interview, and she said:

"Just like a relationship, even in the work environment, instead of getting frustrated with my coworkers because of what they're doing or not doing, I look at the people I work with and say, 'What are their complementary skills that I don't have?' and, 'How do I bring those out in myself and celebrate the differences?' If I get too wrapped up in what people think about me, that's when the stress starts to happen. Really, who cares? You have to live and breathe purpose."

In other words, instead of focusing on what you think about others and their feelings and actions toward you, remain focused on the mission of the organization and on the ways your coworkers contribute to that mission.

Ruggieri also suggests using playful interactions as a way to improve coworker relationships. Ruggieri gave an example of two workers, Amanda, an administrator who wants everyone to follow the rules and do what they're told, and Susie, a salesperson who wants to make lots of sales, even if that means breaking the rules. They butt heads, "But if you tell Amanda and Susie to play *Guitar Hero* for fifteen minutes, they see each other differently." When they are engaged in play, they relate to each other as friends and humans, not coworkers. Ruggieri continued, "It's not that friends aren't going to have disagreements, but the reality is the relationship is more important than disagreement. Friends work through the disagreements and come out even stronger on the opposite side." Sometimes at work, I have forgotten we're all just people, which seems so obvious, but we do have to remind ourselves of this when we're in a nine-to-five routine and feeling the pressure of deadlines or when there's a promotion coming up.

The *Guitar Hero* example doesn't mean you have to hang out with your coworkers all of the time or that you must confide in them. Ruggieri says if you create a sense of "'I actually get where you're coming from,' or, 'I understand why you do this or that,' then that's the magic." A space opens up for you to feel empathy for that other person, so even when they make mistakes or continue to do something that agitates you, you can accept them as they are instead of wishing they would change or be different.

This topic makes me think of something I learned from my dad. If you think someone is about to bad-mouth you in a meeting or a group situation, instead of getting tense and upset, just go sit next to that person. It's extremely awkward talking aggressively and critically about someone when they're so close. This will cause the person to become less aggressive and insulting since they are sitting close to you. You also just might find yourself in a conversation with them, so you have a chance to practice Ruggieri's tips to try and see them as human and look at their point of view, as well as remember what they contribute to the company's mission.

My mom taught me to always be kind and come from a place of love. She is seriously one of the sweetest, kindest people you will ever meet. Hugging her is like sipping on a warm cup of hot cocoa by the fireplace on a cold, wintery night. Her heart is so pure and golden, and you can see her light beaming in the way she smiles. Sometimes, we forget the person across the desk is also a human being with feelings and emotions, a past, and a family. When we start seeing others as humans, our hearts soften a bit, and we can approach the situation from a loving, kind, and compassionate place.

TIPS FOR DEALING WITH COWORKER TENSION

Sometimes, we can adjust our attitudes and then get along with coworkers, but in other cases, that might not be enough. As Susan M. Heathfield writes in her article "How to Deal With a Bully at Work" in *The Balance Careers,* in life, it's usually best to remove yourself from a toxic situation, but that isn't always possible in a workplace situation. Therefore, she argues, "if a coworker is bullying you, sometimes you need to call out this toxic behavior and stand up to it without responding to it on the bully's terms." Heathfield provides a great example of what she means: if someone won't stop criticizing you unfairly in a meeting, don't respond directly or defensively. Instead, ask for direct recommendations from your critic. If they can't come up with any recommendations, their behavior will be revealed as bullying.

Toxic behavior aside, there is a spectrum of responses that are employed in reaction to conflict. According to the article "Conflict Management: Difficult Conversations with Difficult People" by Ann Lowry and Amy Overton, workplace conflict can be incredibly stressful and anxiety-provoking, and they identified several ways people usually cope, depending on the severity of the issue. They find usually the first response is avoidance, including staying silent and ignoring the behavior when it happens. This may be the best method if the issue is minor and can be better fixed by other parties. You have to choose your battles; you don't want to be arguing or fighting over every little issue. So, unless it's something that really bothers and affects you, try to let minor issues go.

Accommodation, the second conflict response Overton and Lowry observed, can be used in a situation where you are in the wrong or if conflict at that moment may be detrimental to broader harmony. This yielding approach may, however, become harmful if the behavior that caused the conflict falls into a pattern of toxicity. For example, if someone takes your stapler and denies it, the easiest road is to get another one from the supply closet. When the thief continues taking things from your desk, the situation could get out of hand to the point they take something actually valuable, and you feel powerless to stop them. The third method the article notes is in direct contrast to the first two: competing, which means responding to conflict by confronting the source of conflict. Competition is a good approach in more dire events and when immediate action is required. What's needed might a be a calm statement of, "That's my stapler you borrowed. If you need your own, there are plenty in the closet."

The last ways Overton and Lowry noticed are compromise and collaboration, which include both opposing parties work together for a resolution. These approaches are similar, but the differences between them are important. In a compromise, the parties have equal power and negotiate; maybe you take turns with the stapler. On the other hand, in collaboration, the focus is broader and on finding a solution in which everyone's needs are met. Perhaps the stapler is moved to a neutral location where everyone can access it freely. Utilizing both of these middle-of-the-road approaches results in problem-solving. This is because of the openness to others' ideas inherent in these solutions, which leads to better outcomes.

I personally like to talk issues out, resolve them, and move on. For instance, once I addressed an issue with a coworker who would take my ideas and present them as her own in team meetings. After the second time she did this, I asked her if we could have a conversation. I rolled my chair over to her desk and got eye level with her.

"I've been noticing you are presenting certain ideas I disclose to you in meetings as your own," I said.

She looked at me with a face of dismay. "What are you talking about? We were discussing it together, and we came up with it together," she said.

I replayed the previous conversation to her for her to realize that no, actually she did not come up with my idea. I concluded the conversation with how I wanted to move forward. "Listen, I am all for collaboration, and we can definitely work together on projects, but it hurts me when my ideas are stolen." From that day on she never presented my ideas as her own again.

Here are a few tips for talking issues out in a respectful manner, all courtesy of the licensed clinical social worker Robert Taibbi from his *Psychology Today* article called "The Art of Solving Relationship Problems." First, use "I" statements, such as: 1) "I feel hurt when you make condescending remarks toward me in team meetings," or 2) "I think it would be wonderful if we could get coffee and do a check-in to make sure I am meeting all my job expectations." These "I" statements are preferable to "you" statements such as, "You are so rude to me during meetings." This is because the "I" statements has you talking about yourself, and your feelings helps keep the other person from feeling like you are blaming or attacking them. This keeps the other person from getting defensive and angry in return.

Another tip is to avoid defensive statements like, "Yes, I did that, but you did x/y/z last week" (Tabbi, 2011). Defensive statements will just add fuel to the fire. If the other person starts getting defensive, try to avoid doing that yourself. Instead, be aware of their feelings and respond strategically. If you think they are getting more upset or sad, ask them in a kind and calm tone, "Did I say something that upset you?" It is best to have a conversation in a calm tone. If you find yourself or the other person getting too heated and the conversation seems like a power struggle, consider calmly saying, "I would like to take a break and reconvene when I have cooled down in an hour." It is helpful to tell the other person when the conversation will continue so it does not leave the other person in limbo (this method also works great in personal relationships with my husband and even my toddler, too).

Active listening is another vital skill for resolving conflicts, and it is the opposite of listening in order to speak, which can further cause friction in a disagreement. Arlin Cuncic describes active listening in *Verywell Mind* as:

"A pattern of listening that keeps you engaged with your conversation partner in a positive way. It is the process of listening attentively while someone else speaks, paraphrasing and

reflecting back on what is said, and withholding judgment and advice."

If you don't pay attention to what your coworker says, it's incredibly difficult to solve the problems you need to work on together—and unless you're planning on leaving your job or avoiding conflict, you'll need to solve your problem.

Overton and Lowry share a formula that might help you remember how to listen actively, which is AMPP: ask, mirroring, paraphrasing, and priming. The goal is to respectfully *ask* what the other person is thinking to spur the conversation into a more productive and empathetic place. Then you describe what you are seeing to hold a *mirror* for them. *Paraphrase* what you've heard. If these steps don't lead you to an understanding, then you're in a good position to *prime* and make an educated guess on what is going on with them so you can decide your next move.

Sometimes you may not be able to work things out with an aggressive or toxic coworker. In these cases, you might have to engage with managers or other leaders to curb toxic behavior. Stav Ziv offers some suggestions in *Themuse Blog* for situations like this. First, it's important to document both your coworker's bad behavior and your own performance: "If you decide to report the bully later, you'll want to be able to give concrete examples of the behaviors you're describing. In addition, start filing away any emails or other evidence to back up your side of the story." For conflicts that need to eventually be mediated by someone else, you'll need evidence on your side. While you arm yourself with facts, Ziv recommends looking up your company's policy on bullying or harassment. If your coworker is violating company policy, you can tell someone in HR or another manager, and they should assist you in finding a solution.

WHEN IT'S A BOSS

The way you deal with a problematic coworker is going to be very different if that coworker is your boss—*yikes*. As an illustration, recall the performance evaluation I shared in this book's introduction. My boss called me out for being late and leaving early, and I felt unable to tell her why. I was afraid of not doing well or performing well and of negative criticism and feedback. Also, there was miscommunication in my hours when I initially started the position and the role lacked clarity. I didn't have much of a backbone at the time to express any of this to my boss, a strong, powerful woman I admired. I would get frustrated by my emotions and was almost afraid of her. It was impossible to show her my vulnerability. This made it difficult to ask for help when I needed it.

Turns out, I wasn't alone in this situation. According to a recent survey by the organizational consulting firm Korn Ferry*, "35% of the respondents say their boss is their biggest source of stress at work, and 80% say a change in leadership, such as a new direct manager or someone higher up the organizational chart, impacts their stress levels." Dealing with a problematic boss can be a lot more complicated than dealing with a problematic peer in the workplace because of the difference in power between you and your boss.

Here's how that power dynamic can play out when you don't agree with a boss. When I asked a coworker, Gina (whose name has been changed to ensure anonymity), what caused her stress at work, she noted it was mostly the way she was managed by her boss and other tensions she had with other coworkers. Frequently, she would argue with coworkers over differences of opinion in team meetings. They never seemed to be able to see eye to eye.

Gina thought her boss gave her an unbalanced amount of negative feedback, sometimes months after something happened. Her check-ins were often skipped or overlooked, and she felt neglected by her boss. Furthermore, when she expressed these frustrations to her boss, nothing changed or was resolved. Gina noticed her boss would not admit when she made mistakes or had flaws; Gina wished her boss would show more vulnerability by expressing her feelings and being more authentic.

She felt bosses should know people come first and should demonstrate their employees' time was valued by not skipping check-ins or meetings. When Gina scheduled meetings or check-ins, her boss would skip the meetings or say they were at unacceptable times. The problem wasn't isolated to Gina; my boss skipped many people's meetings and check-ins. "I felt I did not receive much praise for the good work I did; bosses should not hesitate to value their employees and recognize them when they have done a good job," she told me. Gina added that bosses should give positive and negative feedback in real-time, not wait months after. She also said growth areas should be identified kindly and without ill intent.

Gina was experiencing what researchers call "abusive supervision," and Gina was not alone. Bennet J. Tepper cites findings from *Handbook of Workplace Violence* in his article written in *Journal of Management,* "Abusive Supervision in Work Organizations," which states: "Abusive supervision affects an estimated 13.6% of US workers ... the victims of nonphysical managerial hostility report diminished well-being and quality of work-life that can spill over to their lives away from work." Abusive supervision is still abusive, even if the supervisor doesn't mean to hurt their employees: "A supervisor may mistreat subordinates to elicit high performance or to send the message that mistakes will not be tolerated" (Tepper, 2007). In a separate 2006 article published in *Personnel Psychology,* Tepper discusses findings that businesses lose an astonishing $23.8 billion per year because of abusive supervision. These expensive losses include employee turnover and lost productivity.

The research shows abusive supervision is a serious problem—both for the employees whose mental and emotional health suffers because of abusive supervision and for the companies who lose millions of dollars as a result. How can abusive supervision be fixed? One study published in the *Journal of Managerial Psychology* emphasizes the value of clear communication, since the question of whether subordinates perceive an interaction as abusive depends on both the subordinate and the manager in the situation. Research collaborators Jeremy Brees, Mark Martinko, and Paul Harvey write, "Supervisors might benefit by seeking feedback from subordinates regarding how their feedback delivery is being interpreted to assess and potentially modify their communication style." In other words, it's the supervisor's responsibility to communicate in a considerate way, but it's also the employee's responsibility to tell their supervisor when they said something hurtful. That's easier "said" than done for most of us.

In my case, with therapy, I was able to be honest with my boss about my anxiety and asked for help. I scheduled a check-in meeting with my boss and explained to her why I was late and left early. Through showing her my metrics and that I was still getting my work done although I was not physically in the office, I convinced her I was doing my job. Let your work speak for itself. I reiterated to her I was in therapy and asked if she could be patient with me until I figure it all out. In the end, she surprised me by being kind and understanding—not at all the reaction I had feared.

On the other hand, if you're stuck in a situation where an abusive supervisor refuses to change, it may be time to find a new job or to find a way to change teams or supervisors—because, as the research shows, abusive supervision can have an enormous effect on your mental and emotional health (Tepper, 2007). More about leaving a job will show up in the next chapter when I discuss burnout.

CONCLUSION

Coworkers can be an enormous source of workplace stress and anxiety. In this chapter, I offer suggestions for handling problematic coworkers, including supervisors. Of course, having these kinds of conversations is always easier said than done, but if you develop a thoughtful plan and execute it, your work life can change dramatically. If a problematic coworker refuses to change and they start to greatly impact your well-being, then keep a job change in mind. Changing jobs can be extremely difficult, but sometimes it's the best decision, especially when putting your mental health first. It's important to protect your own mental and social wellbeing. More about what to do when you're considering leaving your job in the next chapter.

CHAPTER TEN

MANAGING BURNOUT

Two days in the office and no one had seen Bella (whose name has been changed to ensure anonymity). No vacation or off-site meetings were on her calendar. Even stranger, no one talked about the fact she was suddenly out. This was so unlike the Princeton alumna who graduated at the top of her class and was very good at what she did. She had just disappeared. Later on, the second day, I stopped one of our coworkers and asked, "Where is Bella?"

"Oh, you didn't hear? She's not feeling well at all. I heard she had a nervous breakdown and even her body was shaking!" my coworker said.

I was shocked. I had just seen Bella the week before, and she seemed completely fine. When she returned to work five days later, I joined her at lunch and asked her how she was doing and what had happened.

She leaned over her veggie sandwich and told me everything. "I was super stressed out, mostly because of work and some other personal issues, but the disappointment and stress I had related to work probably set me over the edge. I had no escape from the stress. Work was not an escape, and neither was home," she said.

"I'm so sorry to hear this," I said. "I had no idea what you were going through."

"I thought I had it under control," she replied, "at least until, as the doctors said, my immune system shut down."

"Wow. How did that feel?" I asked. By then, another coworker had joined us. Everyone in the office was curious about what happened to Bella.

"I don't remember a lot of it, but I was shaking on the floor. I couldn't control my body movements and I couldn't speak. I was crying uncontrollably. Yep, *no bueno.*"

"I was there," someone added. "We were afraid it was a seizure."

Bella had to be rushed to the emergency room after they found her uncontrollably crying and shaking in her office. The cause of her sickness was burnout, and her stress was so great it put her in the hospital. Up until that day, I had never realized burnout was a medical condition, but it is.

The World Health Organization defines burnout on their website as "a syndrome conceptualized as resulting from chronic workplace stress that has not been successfully managed." This syndrome causes employees to feel "depleted or exhausted," "mentally distant from their job," and cynical about their job." In addition, burnout makes employees less effective and diminishes their desires to learn and grow. When employees are experiencing these signs of burnout, most of their energy and mental focus is on daily survival, not on developing for the future.

There are many more stories like Bella's where work is a huge contributor to someone's stress. Even if they are doing a great job, they may not be supported by their leaders with adequate feedback, proper resources, or opportunities to grow. In this chapter, I look at causes of burnout and how it can be prevented. When you know what signs to look for in your work stress, you can tell the difference between normal stress and decide whether it might be time to make a change in your work life—maybe even by changing careers or leaving a job before you pay the price with your health.

CAUSES OF BURNOUT

The causes of Bella's burnout may sound familiar to some readers. Although you don't have to be crying or shaking on the floor to be experiencing burnout. She had felt like the weakest link at work. That was despite her being the first person in her managerial position at the nonprofit startup. She didn't have big shoes to fill; she had to create big shoes herself. She didn't even receive training. Years after her burnout episode, I reached out to her and interviewed her for this book. When I asked what contributed to her burnout, her answer surprised me.

She said, "It was hard! I didn't have easy metrics or best practices to guide me to let me know if I was doing a good job or if I was on the right path." As a result, she just did more and more and more work hoping it would be enough.

Part of the reason Bella was struggling was what experts call "role ambiguity." Simply put, role ambiguity refers to a lack of clarity about a role's expectations. Organizational management consultant Gayatri Patel writes, in her *LinkedIn* article "Role Clarity Is Important to Establish an Effective Team," to avoid role ambiguity, workers should be able to understand what their role is on the team, what is expected of them, how they contribute to the overall vision of the team or organization, what success looks like in their role, and what is at stake if they fail in their role. If you can't answer all of these questions about the role you're currently in, you may be experiencing role ambiguity right now. Role ambiguity is one of the top sources of stress for many employees, according to researcher Thomas Leonard. He writes in "Teams with Role Clarity Are Substantially More Successful than Teams Without" for the *Organizational Diagnostics & Development Oddblog* teams with role clarity are considerably more successful than teams without.

Role ambiguity wasn't the only cause of stress for Bella. She noticed there were inconsistencies and clashes of ideologies in her organization, which led to tension between the leaders and coworkers. She also felt she didn't get adequate constructive feedback from her supervisors. Instead of receiving clear direction from her supervisors, Bella said, "I just came up with organizational tools that worked for me." She wanted feedback from leadership on her role performance, including positive feedback when she was doing well, but she wasn't getting it. The lack of facetime and training from her superiors always made her question whether she was doing a good job. She also felt like she wasn't important because of the lack of interactions and recognition from her boss. On top of all of this, she would be given quick deadlines, and she rarely had enough time to prepare and complete the work without putting in overtime. She says, "I always felt underprepared." What a miserable way to work.

She would feel guilty taking lunch breaks since the culture of the organization frowned upon it. However, she felt she needed to take that hour-long lunch break to get up, move around, go outside, and, of course, to eat. Even though others didn't take their lunch breaks, Bella would. She felt a bit judged by her coworkers who did not take breaks and would ask her when she returned from her lunch break, "Where were you?" So, if she took the lunch break, she increased her stress. If she didn't take it, she also increased her stress.

Getting out of the office for a lunch break can be very important, both for your health and for your productivity. First, and most obviously, you need to eat to function, either physically or cognitively. As Belle Beth Cooper writes in *Fast Company* in 2014, eating a nutritious lunch can "decide your productivity for the rest of the day." On top of that, if you get up, stretch, and walk around during a lunch break, you can avoid pain often associated with desk jobs. Nutrition expert Jackie Middleton writes in a 2019 *Best Health* article that "leaving the office at lunch will stretch your spine and muscles, releasing pressure and eliminating discomfort." There was a scientific basis for Bella feeling better after leaving the office and returning. So, go ahead and take your lunch break!

Bella's lunch breaks were good for her productivity, too. In an interview for NPR, workplace psychologist Kimberly Elsbach says, "Staying inside, in the same location, is really detrimental to creative thinking. It's also detrimental to doing that rumination that's needed for ideas to percolate and gestate." Workplaces that don't make it easy for people to take movement breaks, then, are making their people less effective and maybe even pushing them toward burnout. When working from home, if you're not finding ways to take movement breaks and refresh your scenery, you might be creating your own burnout environment.

"By the time I was close to the end of my time there, when I chose to quit, I was super discouraged," Bella said.

This discouragement partially came from a lack of recognition. I nodded because I had the same experience in that organization.

She continued, "There was this practice of giving praise, which became very isolating because a lot of my work doesn't happen in tandem with everyone else, and not everyone can always see the work I'm doing. So, the people whose [work was] visible always got celebrated the most, and I rarely got recognized."

The pain of being overlooked for praise while she was working so hard made her feel like she was underperforming.

She took it personally, even while she was aware her work was different and would never been seen the way other kinds of work were. Part of her hoped if she finally worked hard enough, she'd be celebrated.

Although she felt alone in her discontent, Bella wasn't the only employee feeling symptoms of burnout—in fact, burnout is alarmingly common. Ben Wigert and Sangeeta Agrawal share some eye-opening statistics in their *Gallup* blog, "Employee Burnout, Part 1: The 5 Main Causes." This recent study of nearly 7,500 full-time employees found 23 percent of employees reported feeling burned out at work very often or always, while an additional 44 percent reported feeling burned out sometimes. That means about two-thirds of full-time workers experience burnout on the job.

These researchers found five factors were strongly correlated with burnout, including unfair treatment at work, unmanageable workloads, unclear work expectations, a lack of communication and support from managers, and unreasonable deadlines (Agrawal, 2018). Interestingly, all of these causes are preventable.

BURNOUT PREVENTION

The good news from Wigert and Agrawal's *Gallup* study is burnout can be prevented and even reversed through appropriate management techniques. They found, "If you don't address the true causes of employee burnout in your organization, you won't have a workplace environment that empowers employees to feel and perform their best."

Employee mental and physical health and business performance both hang in the balance of preventing burnout. As the researchers go on to say, "When employees are running low on high-performance fuel, so are your organization's decision-making, customer service, quality control and innovation engines." It seems then to be in everyone's best interest to get this right.

In another 2021 *Gallup* blog post, "How to Prevent Employee Burnout," researchers conclude managers are largely responsible for the conditions most likely to cause or prevent burnout. They write, "The most immediate way to reduce employee burnout at your organization is for managers and employees to discuss which factors are most relevant to them." Even though there isn't a lot individual employees can do to change burnout conditions, if you're able to create a dialogue with the people in power, you might be able to get the changes you need to do your best work.

Gallup's research emphasizes three areas of improvement that will be relevant to the majority of burnout-inflicted workplaces:

- Wellbeing should be a part of your company's culture. "When wellbeing is an HR-driven nice-to-have rather than the norm modeled across the organization, the workplace culture can perpetuate burnout."
- Organizations need to equip their managers with the tools they need to prevent employee burnout. Ultimately, the employee experience is the manager's responsibility. "It's their duty to set clear expectations,

remove barriers, facilitate collaboration, and ensure that employees feel fully supported to do their best work."

- It's up to managers to figure out what is causing burnout and have an ongoing conversation about the causes of burnout with employees.

If you don't see well-being initiatives, leadership training, or a way to communicate with management, those are signs you could be in a burnout-prone job.

However, even when these issues are addressed, burnout isn't a problem you can fix once. Instead, it's a problem you have to engage consistently. As it turns out, there's no one-size-fits-all solution to the problem of burnout, so the right solution for your workplace will look different than the right solution for a different workplace.

To make matters even trickier, burnout starts at the top and trickles down. The *Gallup* report shows, "many employees who suffer from burnout are managers. . . . Managers report more stress and signs of burnout, worse work-life balance, and worse physical wellbeing than the individual contributors on the teams they lead." This is because managers' positions often come with every-thing that causes employee burnout: lots of work, lots of responsibility, constant distractions, stress, demands, and distractions. Reducing burnout among managers is a key first step to reducing burnout among team members. Look at your boss. Do they seem under stress? Is there a high turnover in leadership positions? They might not be able to help you address your burnout concerns because they can't address their own ("How to Prevent Burnout," 2021).

Ideally, you'll have a leadership team interested in preventing burnout. The *Gallup* study urges business leaders to design the employee experience to be one of low stress and high performance. The term "employee experience" refers to everything an employee goes through in your organization, from getting hired to leaving the organization ("How to Prevent Burnout," 2021). Consider your experience of your job. For the experiences that are unpleasant and stressful, ask yourself, "Could this contribute to burnout? Is there a way to avoid burnout in this situation?" In answering these questions, you could come up with solutions that make you less stressed and a better worker, too.

We don't have to continue burning ourselves out like Bella; the way we're working isn't working. We need to stop glamorizing over-working and seeing business as an indicator of being successful. Many people seem addicted to saying how busy they are and wear it like a badge of honor. They think they sound cool when they say they are busy or life has been hectic. Lack of sleep, relaxation, and time with family and friends is not a sign you are more productive than others. Instead, it's a sign you may be headed for burnout if you don't take steps to prevent it.

ARE YOU GIVING TOO MUCH?

TED podcast host and best-selling author Adam Grant is one of the world's most influential management thinkers and has helped companies like Google, Facebook, Goldman Sachs, and the NBA build healthy workplace cultures. At thirty-seven, he is the highest-rated professor at Wharton, where he earned tenure at twenty-nine. As Emily Goulet says in her *Philadelphia* magazine interview with Grant, his upward mobility is "The academic equivalent of a six-year-old getting a driver's license." He hosts a TEDx podcast and his goal, as he puts it to Goulet, is "to make work not suck" (Goulet, 2018). Turns out, his approach to helping the world is about balancing give and take.

Grant's book *Give and Take: A Revolutionary Approach to Success* argues there are three fundamental styles of social interaction: giving, taking, and matching. Givers in the workplace tilt reciprocity toward giving more than they get. Takers take more than they give, and matchers give and take about the same amount. In Grant's view, success depends on how we approach our interactions with other people to balance these three kinds of interactions.

If you're a taker, you help others strategically—when the benefits to you out-weight the personal costs. If you're a giver, you might use a cost-benefit analysis in which you help when the benefits to others exceed the personal costs, or you might not think about the personal costs at all, helping others without expecting anything in return. If you're a giver at work, you simply strive to be generous in sharing your time, energy, knowledge, skills, ideas, and connections with other people who can benefit from them (Grant, 2013).

We have been taught to succeed—we must compete with others and take what we need. However, recent research and historical evidence show it is not necessarily the takers who win in the end. Those who give reach great heights and create success for others along the way. As Grant argues, a culture of giving in the workplace can lead to greater success, profitability, and productivity as well as happier employees. It can actually improve your emotional and social life at work, decreasing stress and increasing the positive emotions you elicit from others. Givers' networks are vibrant due to their reputations and their willingness to pay forward the help they receive. Successful givers cultivate and use their vast networks to benefit others as well as themselves.

This all sounds great. Being a giver can not only increase your success at work, but it can also ameliorate some of the causes of stress. Though, as Grant emphasizes in *Give and Take*, it's important not to take giving too far. Some givers experience what Grant calls "giver burnout." This burnout isn't caused by giving too much. According to Grant, "Givers don't burn out when they devote too much time and energy to giving.... They burn out when they're working with people in need but are unable to help effectively" (Grant, 2013). The takeaway, then, is being a giver can be immensely beneficial for your work life, but it's important to be a judicious giver to avoid burnout. Avoid giving excessively to people who don't want to receive and find ways to confirm your giving is making a difference.

WHEN IT'S TIME TO GO
"Life is too short to work in a toxic environment." Barry McDonagh told me this in his interview with me. He

encourages employees to talk to their HR department if they are having performance anxiety-related issues, but when you have done everything you can to help yourself, he suggests your job or workplace may not be the best for you. You may have to consider another workplace.

It can be tough to know when it's time to go, and we don't all have the luxury of quitting without having another job lined up. Sometimes planning to leave a job is a long-term affair. McDonagh mentioned you might need to pursue further education. In some cases, people who feel stuck in a particular job have self-esteem and confidence so low they can't imagine they could ever get another job. Still, you can plan your exit to avoid being, as McDonagh says, "Stuck, and when we're caught in situations like that, we cannot see the opportunities. We just see the problem. So that's why talking to other people is beneficial." Talking to a trusted friend, coworker, or career counselor may help you see new possibilities you can't see on your own so you can create your exit.

The thing is, if you know you're on a route to burnout, the healthiest thing you can do might be to walk away. "I don't think people should stay stuck in bad situations." McDonagh continued, "You've got to also look at the career you've chosen and make sure it's aligned with what you really want to do." A career that lacks meaning can cause anxiety and lead to burnout. McDonagh added, "Maybe your career was your parents' idea or society's idea of what a good career is for you, but not what you actually wanted to do."

In those cases, find time to tune into yourself to discover who you really are and what you really want. It's possible that with deep reflection, you might discover you feel stress and anxiety about your work because it's not the right fit for you. Ultimately, the silver lining of experiencing anxiety or even burnout is it could actually help you out of a place you are stuck in and put you back on your path.

CONCLUSION

You don't have to work yourself to burnout to the point of being admitted to the hospital. Notice if your workplace stress and anxiety seem similar to the causes of burnout, like lack of recognition, role ambiguity, poor leadership, and a lack of flexibility in how and when you do your work. There are things you can do and ask your employer to do for you to reduce workplace stress and make the employee experience a priority. Sometimes it's about noticing whether you're giving too much, or if the job is taking too much. If so, you might be able to balance the relationship and avoid burning out. When and if you decide the best thing you can do is walk away from a job, you just might be opening the door to find and fulfill your purpose. More about finding your purpose and other strategies for a positive mindset will come in the next chapter.

CHAPTER ELEVEN

ELEVATE YOUR MINDSET

One of my fears as a young woman was a fear of being pregnant. I had read pregnancy can make your anxiety worse, and I avoided it because I was afraid of postpartum depression and anxiety, nausea, how it would change my body, the lack of sleep (which was an anxiety trigger for me), the change in lifestyle—the list goes on. The worries about what could happen would make me feel nauseous, and I would even throw up. I would cry to my husband and family about my worries—and I wasn't even pregnant.

Yet, more than anything, and despite my anxiety, I wanted to be a mother. My desire to have a baby became larger than my fear, so through some work, reading, therapy, family support, and tools I obtained through the years, I overcame my fear and became pregnant with my firstborn, Rayaan. Spoiler alert: Most of what I had feared never happened. The rest, I handled with ease, and it wasn't that bad at all. As I mentioned earlier, I even earned a yellow belt in karate at thirty-six weeks pregnant! The human body is amazing and is capable of so much more than we think.

Now when my son smiles up at me with his big eyes, when he showers me with kisses and hugs, when I see him laugh and play, I know it was all worth it. It always is. Since then, I gave birth to my second child, my daughter, Amira, who was born in March 2021. I laugh at all the fears I once had. I feel honored to write a book that might help people overcome their fears. I truly believe God only gives you what you can handle, and we are stronger than we think. He gives you strength when you need it. Remembering that will also give you the courage to get through any difficulty. You've gotten through tough times before and you will do it again.

This process I went through might be familiar to many readers even if you aren't mothers or even women. It's common to fear new things and tell yourself all the possible bad things that can happen. This habit of telling yourself negative thoughts can result in a negative mindset that might make you think you "can't" or "shouldn't" do things that are totally doable. Fortunately, if you have a negative mindset, you can interrupt those patterns of thought and reframe them as positive ideas. In my example, I went from being certain every bad thing that can happen in pregnancy would happen to me, and then my mindset shifted. Instead of continuing to feed my fears with negative thoughts, I fed my desire to become a mom with positive thoughts of all the wonderful things I wanted in my life and for my child, and for those to happen, I had to reframe pregnancy. Pregnancy was such a positive experience for me I even picked up karate.

This same shift from negative to positive can also happen with fears and anxieties that arise in the workplace, and in this chapter, I will share a few tips that apply in both scenarios. We should be aware of a fixed mindset that makes you lower your expectations versus a growth mindset in which you increase your expectations—and we often get what we expect. It may be that understanding your purpose more fully will lead to a change to a more positive mindset. It's amazing to see what's possible in life and work when you choose the higher thought.

ANTICIPATE THE GOOD

During my first pregnancy, I was experiencing what psychologists call "anticipatory anxiety." According to Srini Pillay's article "Anticipatory Anxiety: The Suffering and Solutions" in *Psychology Today*, "Anticipatory anxiety is a negative projection of an unknown outcome." In other words, it's when you assume, without evidence, things are going to go wrong. Consider this: if you've never asked for a raise and feel a rush of reasons not to ask for one just by thinking about it, you might be experiencing anticipatory anxiety. Same thing if you feel unable to disagree or say no to people and considering doing so leaves you paralyzed and in mortal fear. Just like other forms of anxiety, anticipatory anxiety can be harmful, not just in the effects of the stress, but also in your job mobility and performance.

One way to navigate anticipatory anxiety and worrying is to notice moments when a fearful emotion or thought arises. For instance, your boss asks you to work this weekend, and you have a wedding to attend. This question might cause you anxiety if you feel unable to say no and fear looking like a poor team player. When you isolate that moment, you can shift the fear by breaking the cycle with a positive thought. You can say, for example, "What if I tell my boss I'm going to an event this weekend, and they say okay?" If you can't think of anything positive, try looking at positive images like cute dog or cat memes and videos or listening to positive music. This almost always works. "Learn how to convert anticipatory anxiety into hope, the positive anticipation of an unknown outcome. Positivity not only reflects reality, but it also creates reality" (Pillay, 2011). Don't wait until the anticipatory anxiety is over—interrupt it.

Another tool to stave off anticipatory anxiety is to stay in the present. When you find yourself worrying about something, like whether or not your boss will ask you to work on the weekend, it can be easy to daydream the worst-case scenario for no reason and become more upset when nothing has happened. Stay in the present by saying to yourself, "I will worry about it when I *have* to worry about it. Everything is okay right now." Stay in the present moment and then go about your day; keep repeating as necessary. Usually, 99 percent of the worries and fears we have never actually manifest; it's all just our mind creating stories.

To bring yourself back to the present moment, ask yourself: what is happening right here, right now? Look around you and remind yourself where you are. Take in the environment with your five senses. What do you see, smell, taste, hear, feel? Intentionally shifting your attention can be a valuable tool, as Srini Pillay suggests: "Rather than focus on your heartbeat that is getting faster and faster or doing something that is just going to go along with that (like surfing the net), change your attention to something completely different." Once you're fully present, the worry may just disappear so you can focus on the present task.

When you're in transition or anticipating change and fears and worries are popping into your mind left and right, you might choose to set aside a "Worry Time." Set a time in the day, about ten minutes, when you are free to do all the worrying you want. You can even write all of your worries in your journal during your worry time. When you worry outside of this time, remind yourself to wait until your worry time. This frees up the rest of your time to do your best work in a focused way or even enjoy the time you're not at work.

FIXED/GROWTH MINDSET

In the midst of my pregnancy anxiety, I had a fairly negative mindset. I would always think the worst, expect the worst, and prepare for the worst. I would constantly wonder why I had such bad anxiety, asking *why is this happening to me* and thinking the world was against me. I used to hate the feelings and sensations of anxiety. I would fight those feelings. I had a *fixed* mindset, in which I felt things would never change, and I would always have anxiety. This was my life, I thought. However, through therapy and reading many self-help books I realized having a *growth* mindset was much more productive. People with growth mindsets acknowledge they are dynamic and can grow and change.

In her book *Mindset: The New Psychology of Success*, Stanford psychologist Carol Dweck affirms the importance of growth and fixed mindsets: "Out of these two mindsets, which we manifest from a very early age, springs a great deal of our behavior, our relationship with success and failure in both professional and personal contexts, and ultimately our capacity for happiness." Interestingly, the words or ideas we tell ourselves shape a great deal of our mindsets. So, it is important to be aware of your self-talk language.

The way you word things to yourself can change your mindset. For instance, instead of saying, "I am not good at public speaking," you could say, "I am not good at public speaking *yet*." The second phrase implies that with enough work, you could become a great public speaker, thereby emphasizing your ability to grow and change.

This shift to a growth mindset can even work when you have a setback. As Maria Popova writes for *Brainpickings.com* in 2014, the growth mindset sees failure as an opportunity for growth, not as a sign of unintelligence. Imagine the freedom to know you can only learn and grow from your failures, instead of beating yourself up about it.

In addition to what we think we can or can't do, the fixed/growth mindset often arises when we look at what we don't have and instead look at what others have. While we are feeling anxious at work, we see others on lavish vacations, and it may make us feel jealous and resentful. Social media often makes this stress worse.

We are constantly seeing the highlight reel of other people's lives and comparing them to our reality. What you see on social media is only a snippet of someone's life, not all of it. We compare our worst to someone's best, and that's when we start to feel less about ourselves. My mom, Unsar Tahira, always told me to never look at people who have more than I do but always to be grateful for what I have. She taught me to be grateful because you never know you could lose those things or people you take for granted. If we change our mindset and be appreciative instead of envious, then we will be happier.

ACCEPT AND ALLOW

Although the fixed versus growth mindset is vitally important, it's not the only way to think about how your mindset affects your response to stress or anxiety. I spoke about this topic with Michelle Cavanaugh, a licensed clinical social worker (LCSW) and anxiety coach in the D.A.R.E. program. In fact, she was my anxiety coach, so I was excited to share with my readers her expert advice that helped me.

Although everyone's anxiety is rooted in different situations and circumstances, Cavanaugh notes anxiety treatment is very general no matter the problems. Everyone has complex and diverse fears that manifest in different ways. Everyone also feels as though their anxiety is different from other people's anxiety. Cavanaugh explains fighting anxiety is very general; it is all about accepting and allowing. She says:

"We're all humans, we all basically work the same; we all process things the same and are put together similarly. We have an internal alarm that goes off when it senses energy to fight that thing. We are all just fighting different things."

Ironically enough, fighting anxiety is all about learning how not to fight what you're feeling. Instead, you're changing what those feelings mean, which is another way of adjusting your mindset.

There will always be stressors at work, and stressors are completely normal, but some people view these stressors as things that *have* to get done or *need* to be perfect. According to Cavanaugh, people create extra stress levels just by coming up with ideas of problems in their head—for example, the need to be perfect or the need for someone to like you. These thoughts are just extra stress your mind is adding to the task.

Cavanaugh discusses the significance of changing your mindset. She emphasizes for people who feel anxiety, "there is nothing actually wrong with us; the only thing that is wrong with us is that we start fighting our anxiety." That's why in my TEDx Talk I encourage you to "go spaghetti" and not fight your anxiety and let it run its course.

I found it helpful to choose one main mantra to focus on when you are feeling anxious. The reason is when you are feeling very anxious, it can be quite hard to focus on the task at hand and remember all of the tips and tricks to perform it well. This is why I used to keep my favorite mantras written in my "notes" on my phone so I could just read them whenever I needed. One of my favorite mantras for focus is "just sit with it," which is basically to accept and allow all feelings to come and to go. Sometimes it's as simple as that. Other mantras that work for me include: "But did you die?" "It be like that sometimes," and, "It is what it is, just go with the flow!" These make me laugh and break the seriousness of the mood.

One way to work with your mindset to cooperate with anxiety is to speak in definitive statements. For example, common anxiety-producing statements include: "I have to do X to overcome my anxiety," or "I'll only be happy if I accomplish this goal by my birthday," etc. You do not *have* to do anything in your life. Happiness and calmness can happen anywhere and at any time. You don't need to attain anything to get to that goal. The core method of treating anxiety is accepting your feelings and the circumstances while not fighting yourself and your feelings. The anxiety-producing statements above can be reframed to be more calming like, "I can overcome my anxiety whether I do X or not," or, "I'll be happy on my birthday whether I accomplish this goal or not." See the difference? Cavanaugh clarifies anxiety will not disappear when you rewrite those statements, but doing so can ease anxiety so it does not cause problems in your life anymore.

You don't always have the power to choose how to feel about the situations you find yourself in, like facing a deadline at work that has real consequences if you fail. You do have some agency, though. You are not completely helpless or completely beholden to the way your situation makes you feel. You have the power to change which feelings you focus on, and you have the power to contextualize the things that happen to you in a particular way.

Often, when a "negative" situation occurs, such as not getting that promotion for which you have been working so hard, we feel awful, but we also feel we *shouldn't* feel awful. You may think, "I shouldn't feel sad right now. At least I have a job. I don't want to feel this." Why shouldn't you? Of course, you should feel sad. You didn't get that promotion you wanted. It is normal to feel sad, so let yourself feel. It is okay not to be okay. Humans are funny in that way. Sometimes we feel numb, and we wish we felt more, and other times we want to be numb and not feel anything because it is too intense for us.

Mark Manson discusses accepting one's feelings in his book *The Subtle Art of Not Giving a F*ck*. He states, "The desire for more positive experience is itself a negative experience. And, paradoxically, the acceptance of one's negative experience is itself a positive experience." In other words, the healthiest response for us is to let ourselves feel what we need to feel fully. It will come, and it will go. Don't wish away your negative feelings. Don't wish to feel better in a situation where you clearly need to be sad (e.g., if a loved one passes away). I know this can be difficult when all you see on social media is everyone having the time of their lives, which makes us feel there is something wrong with us, when in reality we are just having normal human feelings.

On the other hand, if we were super happy all the time, then people would look at us weird, and we may even be considered "manic." If you think about it, it's not normal to be super happy all the time. So, feel all the feelings and keep on movin' on. To feel is to be human. It means you are alive. Embrace that, and don't be afraid of your feelings, don't fight them, and just let them be. When you accept and allow your emotions, even fear and anxiety, you stay in control of your actions and reactions.

RUGGIERI'S SIX-STEP PROCESS TO A PURPOSEFUL LIFE

In some cases, the negative emotions and talk in your mind might be a signal you're not on a path to fulfill your purpose, as McDonagh mentions in the last chapter. Instead of reframing the negative statements into positive ones, you might consider if the solution is to take actions that are more in alignment with your purpose. That's easier said than done for most of us. Fortunately, Jess Ruggieri, the management expert you met in Chapter Five, shared a six-step process to living a purposeful life with me when I interviewed her. She outlines a process to establish your purpose, prioritize your activities, plan your goals, pursue them, take care of yourself, and purge what's no longer serving you. Below, I outline each step in detail.

First, Ruggieri suggests you establish your personal purpose and, "make sure your personal purpose aligns with your professional priorities." So, if you care deeply about the environment and work in a job that has a lot of waste, you might be out of that alignment. On the other hand, if you are passionate about children's well-being and have a job that allows you to impact children in a positive way, you are in alignment. As Ruggieri suggests, the key is to "establish . . . your personal purposes and then find the right organizational culture to match. Find an organization that will allow you to live out your personal purpose, and then [make] sure the job they're asking of you aligns with that." Imagine how fear, stress, and anxiety around the workplace can drastically reduce when you're confident your projects are giving purpose to your life. This also makes it much easier to have a positive mindset because there's little friction between what you're doing and what you feel inspired to do.

Once you've established your purpose, use that purpose to determine what you need to do and what you don't need to do. "Prioritize, right?" Ruggieri told me. "Decide what stays and what goes because some things you have to eliminate." You can't do everything, so you should focus on doing those things that advance your purpose. Often, the activities that give us stress or anxiety are not advancing our purpose, which can create a negative mindset, such as feeling like there's no reason to do what you're doing, so you feel worthless. When you stop prioritizing those activities, you'll have more room for meaningful projects that make you feel like you and your contribution are valuable.

Ruggieri's third step is to plan. Write down a plan to fulfill your purpose and commit to it. However, don't just say, "I'm going to change careers." Make sure your plan is reasonable and reasonably paced. As Ruggieri says, if you have "a long-term goal, then you know it's a long process, but you have to start somewhere. It's developing habits, and you have to enjoy the journey." Setting unrealistic goals can set you up for more anxiety, as Ruggieri told me. "If I put a deadline on myself and it's not realistic . . . I put the stress in my own freaking life and I forget the fact that I designed that for myself." Often, as stress and anxiety can come up in the course of goal planning, you can address those concerns in your plan to remain calm and focused. So, if a fear about your career change is your resume could be stronger, add to the plan to edit your resume and work with a consultant or coach. This strategy will help you stay in a positive mindset while creating your plan.

Once you've set your goals, it's time to pursue them. Nothing will change unless you get started, maybe even today. If plans are not turned into action, nothing changes. You can't stop at the planning stage. You have to move forward and execute your plan. As you take action toward your goal, stay in a positive mindset because anxiety and stress often appear when you're making a change, so keep referring to all the tools in this chapter and the next one to stay confident and on track.

The next step is to remember you are engaging in a process and a practice, not a single effort that either will or won't work. At the first sign of failure or when success isn't immediate, sometimes people will abandon their plan. Don't let that be you. Your plan needs to stay healthy and sustainable, so give yourself a break. You need to recognize things take time, so keep at it. Ruggieri reminded me here to play with different ideas and enjoy the journey of pursuing purpose.

Her final step is to purge or stay organized and get rid of stuff that is getting in the way of progress. Ruggieri says, "I don't even have a junk drawer. Everything in my [home] has a purpose and a place it resides in for a reason." That's how your work environment should be, too, and you can use the tools in Chapter Seven to reduce your clutter. Then, you can do as Ruggieri says and, "set yourself up a space that is purposeful. [Think about] what's going to make you happy and don't sit around complaining about the environment; make it happen!" For many of us, getting rid of physical clutter isn't as hard as another kind of clutter: people who aren't lifting you up.

If your present company is not providing you what you need, you may have to remove yourself, even if they are relatives. Then, Ruggieri says, "Seek out a friend . . . somebody within your work environment and ask them to go for a five-minute walk or if they want to grab lunch. . . . It's risky because people can say no or reject you," but asking can help you develop self-confidence. If you struggle to find human connections at work, consider creating moments to organically connect with people. One way to do that is to extend invites to people to talk and walk or to grab coffee. If you are not physically in a location with coworkers, you can always set up fifteen-minute "coffee over Zoom" meetings just to talk about non-work-related topics. These small moments of human connection can greatly benefit your wellbeing and experience at work.

These new, positive relationships can also fill the gaps the old relationships weren't filling.

CHOOSING THE HIGHER THOUGHT

When it comes to mindset, we get to choose if we continue with a negative mindset or instead choose a positive mindset, no matter what we are facing. Terri Levine, chief Heart-repreneur® and mentoring expert at heart-repreneur.com, said to me in her interview, "We get to choose our thoughts in every moment, and if our self-talk is, 'Oh no, this isn't going to go well,' or, 'I'm so anxious,' or whatever it is, we're going to create more of that, and we're going to show up like that." As a result, that anxiety and what we fear is the thing people will see and believe about us. To avoid this, Levine suggests exerting agency over your own thoughts. The first step is to "just notice it. Don't beat yourself up. Notice it, observe it, witness it, and then choose a thought that is a little bit better than that." These incremental shifts can create a big change as you keep choosing the higher thought and say, "I will do my very best at this."

Levine further explained people can choose their mindset, which is a process she has learned and applied in her own life. She said:

"I used to choose what [are] called firefighting thoughts. Everything was a problem. It was a fire that, somehow, I had to put out. Then, when I got really aware of that, [I] made a choice to be very conscious and go, 'Okay Terri, you're going into that mode again. Breathe, get centered, take it slow.'"

Over time, as she would think differently in the firefighter moments, she shifted her mindset. She kept reframing her self-talk until those anxiety-producing incidents no longer triggered an anxiety response from her. She was in control of herself, no matter what happened externally.

Over practice, higher thoughts become new learned behaviors. "Get conscious of your thoughts and start to take responsibility for choosing something," Levine says. For example, if you're in traffic and find yourself getting irritated or frustrated, chose to enjoy that time by playing music, listening to a podcast, making a phone call, or listening to an audiobook you might enjoy. You can't control that situation, so don't resist it. Listen to your self-talk and breathe. If you are late, you are late; it's not the end of the world. Changing your perception about a situation by being conscious of your thoughts and nudging them toward a more positive worldview will make an incredible difference in your stress levels. It's really empowering to know you get to choose that next thought.

Levine told me about a tool she uses and recommends to her clients to help with negative thoughts: the rubber-band technique. If your head is racing with negative thoughts, snap a rubber band against your skin. "It should hurt a little bit so you wake yourself up, you change your neurological state," so you can literally *snap out of it* and choose a more positive thought. Marking negative thoughts with the sting of a rubber band can help you realize how much time you give those thoughts. "It really works," Levine exclaimed, "Because you're like,

'Oh boy, there I go again. Let me stop. There I go. Let me stop.'" Then, you can reset your mindset toward the higher thought.

I used the rubber band method when I was pregnant with my first child and constantly having negative "what if" thoughts. Using the rubber band method helped me become aware of my thoughts. I used the method to bring me back to the present moment and then conscientiously chose a higher thought.

CONCLUSION

There are many ways to work with your mindset to expect and believe the best outcomes are imminent. It's possible to work with your anxiety to anticipate the best outcomes instead of the worst to maintain a positive mindset. Sometimes when fears and anxiety around tasks and projects arise, the culprit may be a fixed mindset, which you can shift to a positive one, which will help you stay on track. The best course of action when anxiety arises may be to accept and allow it to run its course. Maybe those unpleasant emotions and the negative self-talk are telling you to do something else instead to fulfill your purpose. No matter what happens, you can always choose the higher thought. These practices may not guarantee everything you do will be an absolute success, but they will help you feel great about yourself and your future even when setbacks arise. In the next chapter, I provide a variety of stress management habits to use throughout the day, so you stay in control of how you feel.

CHAPTER TWELVE

STRESS MANAGEMENT HABITS IN ACTION

With your positive mindset, as you manage stress and anxiety, there's room for something else to emerge—happiness and joy. "Happiness doesn't just happen. You make it happen. The thoughts, beliefs, and behaviors you choose have a tremendous impact," said Theresa Bodnar, a lieutenant colonel in the US Army Reserve and certified Army Master Resilience Trainer (MRT). When I interviewed her, we explored what's complicated about discussing "happiness." If you're overwhelmed and miserable in work or life, you just want to feel better, and it might not even seem possible to get all the way to happiness.

Not to mention "happiness" means different things to different people. For Bodnar, happiness is having a balanced life. Her idea of balance used to vacillate between high and low periods, with very little rest in between. That lifestyle was neither healthy nor useful, and it was very stressful for her. When she realized she was lacking balance, she stopped trying to do everything and chose something different for her health and wellbeing—to put them first.

For me, happiness is about being grateful for what you have in life and being content. My mom always told me to be grateful for even the little things such as the ability to see, hear, taste, and having working hands and feet. I am healthy, I have roof over my head, and food to eat. Studies show after our basic human needs are met such as food, water, shelter, and financial security, more money does not necessarily make us happier. For example, Belinda Luscombe wrote in *Time* about a Princeton study that found once people make more than $75,000 per year, more money doesn't increase their happiness. If you make more than about $75,000, more money probably won't make you happier. I would argue what will make you happier is applying stress management habits to regulate your emotions and fears so you can choose how you want to feel no matter what is happening in your life or at work.

There's a cult of daily habits in our society that says you need to work out, write, and meditate every day. These daily habits are not necessarily the way to managing stress for all of us, although exercise, journaling, and meditation certainly work for some people. Stephen King says in his book *On Writing* that to write a book, one must only write five hundred words a day. Duh, sounds so easy . . . especially if that's your full-time job.

The problem is when you have a goal to do your daily habits and miss a day or a few days, you can feel disappointed with yourself and decide to stop trying. Strict schedules aren't a prerequisite for doing great work, so that's not what I mean by daily habits. If you miss a day or two, don't be hard on yourself and just jump back into the routine the next day. You know yourself best. University College of London Professor Philippa Lally and associates in *European Journal of Social Psychology* found, "missing one opportunity to perform the behavior did not materially affect the habit formation process." If you are the type who's hard on yourself, give yourself more grace. If you are like me and are often lenient with yourself, be firmer (but always kind). You have to find what works best for you.

Still, daily habits can be a powerful tool for achieving any life goal, including reducing your work-related stress. So, in this chapter, I offer a narrative of a healthy workday, emphasizing the most powerful habits you can use to diminish your work-related stress. Remember: even if you don't do every single one of these habits every single day, you can still improve! Adopt just one habit at a time if that works better for you. Health psychology lecturer Benjamin Gardner and fellow researchers posit in *British Journal of General Practice* that every time you apply the change and repeat the action, new mental links are formed, which is called "context-dependent repetition." Basically, our brain saves energy because by just doing the same things every day those actions become second nature so we don't have to think about them.

You may have heard the myth that it takes twenty-one days for a habit to form. Gardner shows, however, it takes around sixty-six days—nine weeks or so—to form a new habit. So, don't be discouraged if you take a couple of months to form a habit. Just keep at it. On the other hand, podcaster Scott Smith notes in his "Breaking Habits Now or Later" episode on *Daily Boost* that research has also shown if you are truly committed and make a stern decision to do something, you can create a new habit instantly!

Good habits start with celebrating one successful day, moment, or activity. Then the next and the next.

THE MORNING ROUTINE

When you wake up, smile big. Be thankful for another new day and a fresh new start. It's a blessing to be alive. Express gratitude for the day, or practice prayer. Every morning when I wake up, I always say, "It's a beautiful morning!" I say this even if it's rainy and gloomy outside, even if I don't feel like smiling, I just do it anyway and it becomes a habit. This way I start my day on an *oomph.* I have even noticed my son now also starts his day by saying, "It's a beautiful morning!" Besides setting good habits for ourselves, it is important to model that behavior for our children since they do most of their early learning through observation.

After you get out of bed, consider taking a cold shower instead of a hot shower. The primary contemporary proponent of cold therapy, Wim Hof, has devised a method for using cold to improve your life. On the "Cold Therapy" page on *WimHofMethod.com* Hof claims cold therapy can burn fat, improve sleep, decrease inflammation, and provide a boost to your immune system, and he has sponsored scientific research that supports his claims. These studies have shown cold water improves your immune system and your body's ability to handle stress. So even thirty seconds of cold water at the end of your shower will help. Turn the knob all the way to the cold side, and for a bonus, cold water also closes up your pores.

As you brush your teeth, do your makeup, and/or shave, listen to some affirmations. Think that sounds too easy? Actually, there's a lot of scientific support for affirmations, as Christopher N. Cascio writes in 2016 publication of *Social Cognitive and Affective Neuroscience.* He explains affirmations activate our reward circuits and can help decrease pain and improve our responses to stress. You can find lots of affirmations on YouTube—just play the video using the phone speaker as you get ready.

I recommend "I AM" by Jason Stephenson. I listen to these almost every morning while getting ready. Stephenson has many different types of affirmation videos, which affirm inner strength and power, abundance, and other positive outcomes. If affirmations feel awkward for you or you feel you are lying to yourself, you can try repeating, "I am committed to improving myself." You might also consider listening to uplifting or motivational music— and even dancing—while you get ready. This can motivate you to tackle the day head-on.

Another great habit for mornings is meditation, which helped me calm my obsessive, non-stop thoughts. When you first start, it's hard, so I recommend guided meditation.

I got an app called Calm and bought the yearly subscription. Honestly, it helped me a lot. Once you meditate for a while and keep reminding yourself to stay in the present moment, you will notice a big difference. My thoughts slowed down, and I was even sleeping better.

As I explain in Chapter Three, exercise and nutrition choices are important for reducing stress. You can start both of those good habits in the morning. Exercise, even a light yoga or dance session in the morning, can help reduce your anxiety. Just get your blood pumping.

Remember to eat a nutritious breakfast like eggs and toast, something with protein and carbohydrates. Carbs provide fast energy and protein provides prolonged energy. Bella, who you met in Chapter Ten and who experienced burnout, emphasized the importance of eating healthy to help her anxiety. "Food is mood!" she exclaimed. The irony is when we don't feel well, we want junk food. Junk food can increase anxiety, especially sugary foods, caffeine, alcohol, etc. However, in stressful moments, that's really when we should be eating healthy to help boost our mood. The healthier you eat when you are anxious or depressed, the better you will feel. Magnesium supplements have been proven to help with anxiety.

While you're focused on being diligent, remember to have a good time, too. Do something you enjoy in the morning. I love watching *Hoda and Jenna* (formerly *Kathie Lee and Hoda*) while I eat my breakfast. You might prefer some other activity, just make sure you're experiencing some pleasure and joy before you start your productive day.

Walking out the door, say to yourself, "Something wonderful is going to happen today." Then ask yourself why and how. Your brain will start searching for answers. Where your focus goes, energy flows. If you focus on having a great day, then you most likely will have a great day. This positive focus exercise will set you up to enjoy your commute as much as you can. (You might consider working a different shift or even moving if your commute consistently causes a severe amount of stress). Listen to podcasts, audiobooks, or some bumpin' music. Don't get frustrated by traffic; accept and allow it. Don't resist your reality; that will cause suffering.

Now, with COVID-19, many of us don't have a commute anymore. However, it will still help to get up and do your normal (or enhanced) routine, such as getting ready for the day, putting on makeup if you like, eating breakfast, getting your coffee or tea, and then heading to your laptop, desk, or office.

THE WORKDAY ROUTINE
You can be thoughtful and intentional about every part of your day. For example, consider how you feel when you walk into the workplace (or when you log on to your computer). Do you greet friendly coworkers who know you, or do you silently begin work among strangers? Obviously, entering into a warm and welcoming workplace where you have meaningful connections with others is the preferable option. So, make meaningful connections at work.

Once you begin work, there are a number of things you can do to make work as relaxed as possible. They include stop-drop-and-roll, organization, taking breaks, challenging yourself, asking for help, controlling your space, practicing awareness, stop-drop-and-roll, the easy button, and gratitude.

STOP, DROP, AND ROLL

I have developed my own de-stressing technique that works really well for me. I call it "stop, drop, and roll," which you might recognize from fire drills. Use this in moments when you notice your body language signaling stress. If you are feeling stressed, you may find yourself clenching your fists, tightening your shoulders, clenching your jaw, and furrowing your eyebrows and forehead. To de-stress, relax all of those muscles—go spaghetti! By relaxing your muscles, you send a signal to your brain that you are not stressed or feeling anxious.

Here are the three steps:

Stop: Take a pause from what you're doing and take three deep belly breaths. Picture a stop sign. You can even put your hand out in the stop signal.
Drop: Drop your shoulders. While taking deep breaths, relax the muscles in your face, including your jaw, eyes, and forehead. Even drop your tongue from the roof of your mouth.
Roll: Roll your shoulders back. Do a little roll dance; let the sensations pass through you. Accept them and let them be there. Just sit with the feelings; they will pass.

Once they do, smile! Go spaghetti! When you're feeling anxious, you can even say, "Uh oh! Spaghetti-o!" and go limp like a spaghetti. This will make you laugh and lighten the mood.

BE ORGANIZED

Staying organized can keep symptoms of stress and anxiety at bay, as I explored in Chapter Seven. Filing and clearing your desk and computer desktop may rank low on your priority list, but they can save you time in the long run and may prevent a crisis later.

I want to live my life by design, not by default, so everything I do goes on my calendar, even lunch meetings or hanging out with my friends, but especially my work tasks. Make to-do lists and prioritize your work and schedule with enough time to complete each task or project. In addition, get started on major projects as early as possible and set mini deadlines for yourself. This allows you to anticipate problems and work to prevent them. With your schedule created, use your alerts and reminders to keep yourself on track. That way, you're in control of how you want to spend your time. Don't forget to prioritize taking breaks. Set reminders on your phone or set out blocks in your calendar.

Being able to effectively manage your workload is important for reducing work-related stress and improving productivity, which is why Bodnar uses task-management activities. We feel stress when our workload exceeds our perceived capacity to complete assigned tasks. For Bodnar, writing to-do lists, prioritizing tasks for herself and her team, and aggressively managing her calendar are effective task management activities she implements daily. Bodnar has also learned the art of gracefully saying "no" when she has too much to do. As Stephen Covey says in his book *The 7 Habits of Highly Effective People,* "Rather than always focusing on what's urgent, learn to focus on what's really important." These tips are important for keeping your time and activities organized and decreasing your work stress.

TAKE BREAKS

Exercise is nature's anti-anxiety/depression medicine. It increases blood flow so you will think better at work and have more energy; it improves mood, promotes better sleep, controls weight, and helps combat disease and health conditions. To take advantage of the benefits of exercise, take breaks throughout the day to walk around, even if you're only walking around inside. You might also have walking meetings. The deep breathing cardiovascular exercise might induce can help clear your head. You don't need to earn a break, you deserve it.

You might also take mindfulness breaks to connect with the present moment and induce relaxation. When you know you are being triggered by someone or something at work, walk away, take a few minutes to do some deep breathing exercises to calm yourself, think through the issue rationally, and then re-engage. Mindfulness breaks are also just a great healthy work habit in general. In addition to engaging in deep breathing exercises, unplugging from technology regularly has been shown to support overall health and wellbeing, improve cognitive functioning, and lower stress levels.

Back-to-back meetings can be stressful and draining, so Bodnar has developed a technique she calls "the intentional meeting." To have intentional meetings, set meeting times with five minutes to spare—twenty-five-minute meetings, fifty-five-minute meetings, and so on. This way, if you have back-to-back meetings, you will always have five minutes for yourself to decompress, get refocused, do some deep breathing exercises, or take a bathroom break.

Don't feel guilty about taking breaks to recharge and rejuvenate yourself. Building "gap time" into your day is essential to managing stress. Dr. Daniel Kirsch, president of the American Institute of Stress, recommends building in five "gaps" a day. Kellie Marksberry paraphrases his advice in her article "Top 5 Workplace Stress Busting Tips" for *The American Institute of Stress*. Kirsch's gaps include: one when you wake up, one at ten o'clock in the morning, two o'clock in the afternoon, four o'clock in the afternoon, and again at bedtime. Each gap is an opportunity to check in with yourself and to observe how you're doing. You might choose to ask yourself how you are doing. After all, you can only take action to prevent or mitigate stress if you understand it's happening to you.

CHALLENGE YOURSELF

Challenging yourself at work, doing purposeful and meaningful work, and finding opportunities to grow is an ongoing theme for finding happiness in the workplace. "If work did not give me opportunities to grow, I would create them myself and present them to my boss. Also, learn to advocate for yourself," said Bedford in her interview.

Challenging yourself and growing outside of the workplace can be a big help, too. Hands-on hobbies like cooking, gardening, woodworking, and crafting can improve your happiness. Kelly Lambert writes in *Lifting Depression: A Neuroscientist's Hands-on Approach to Activating Your Brain's Healing Power,* our ancestors used to do these kinds of activities to survive, so our brains release serotonin and dopamine when we engage in hobbies.

IF YOU NEED HELP, ASK

Learn to ask for help if you need it. Simon Sinek, one of the most influential voices in the leadership world, said in a presentation during Usher's New Look Disruptive Innovation Summit, "The single most valuable thing you ever will learn in your entire life is to accept help when offered and to ask for help when you know you can't do it." Take advantage of employer-provided resources and benefits, including vacations. Your workplace may offer an employee assistance program (EAP), discounts to gyms, or skill-building courses. Find out what's available to you.

I struggled with asking for help whether it was help with my kids or help at work. However, when I got to a point of almost burning out, I had no choice but to ask for help. Before, I wouldn't ask for help because it made me feel like I was perhaps not good enough or competent enough to take care of the things I needed to take care of. I was also always afraid of looking weak or worried about whether they said no. We also don't ask for help because we believe we can do it better than anyone else, which *may* be true, but what you will find is even if the person does the job half as good as you, it is still helpful! So, when I was at my wits' end, I finally hired someone to assist me with my kids, which made a world of difference—heck, it enabled me to finish writing this book! I can't emphasize this enough: ask for help, and you won't be sorry! We weren't meant to do it all.

CONTROL YOUR SPACE

For those who suffer from anxiety, we all know too well that we like to always be in control—of everything. When we feel a loss of control, that causes us a lot of anxiety. "We're calmest when we have a territory we can control—and having control of our experiences boosts performance and reduces stress," says Sally Augustin, an environmental-design psychologist, in an interview with Claire Burke for a 2016 *Guardian* article. This can be easier said than done if you work in an office with an open floor plan. Augustin suggests a number of strategies for controlling your territory.

You might put large plants around your desk or on your desk that obstruct your view of coworkers sitting nearby. Buy good noise-canceling headphones. Have lunch outside of the office. If people can approach you from behind, maybe keep a mirror on your desk so you're not caught unaware. Take breaks to leave the office space and get a breather, and remind yourself everyone is in the same boat. Reminding yourself of this truth may not change the situation, but it can make you feel solidarity with your coworkers, which is the main point of an open office anyway.

Be aware of how seeing others in the space affects you, like how coworkers conversing without you could leave you feeling left out and upset. To cope with that anxiety, ask yourself, "What story am I telling myself about this situation?" Often, it's not personal, even though we always tend to take it personally. Our imagination creates embellished stories about why we were not invited. "Maybe you're worried you're not valued, or your job is at risk," says Laurie Cameron, author of *The Mindful Day*. "Many of our fears aren't based on objective reality. To feel calm, put your hand on your heart and say to yourself, 'You're okay. Everyone feels like this sometimes.'" In these ways, you take control of your space and how other people in the space impact your levels of stress.

PRACTICE AWARENESS

Control your thoughts, more or less, by practicing awareness. To do so, you first need to be aware of your thoughts, especially the negative self-talk. The second step is to interrupt those thoughts and replace them with a more positive thought. For example, you may catch yourself saying, "I am a loser." You need to interrupt that thought by saying, "Stop!" or picturing a stop sign and then replacing it with a positive thought like, "I am worthy, I am enough!" If you are self-critical and have many negative thoughts about yourself or internalize what others say about you, write down affirmations to rebut those thoughts. Remember the words of others are just opinions and not true facts. Someone can call you a loser, but that doesn't mean it's true. Do not take what people say personally; what they say is often a reflection of their own personal issues (unless you really did something messed up, then take responsibility for it).

The real trick is to be able to allow your thoughts to come and go and not be bothered by them or react to them. Sometimes it is better to not try to "control" them but just let them be and keep on living your life. For instance, the more I tell you not to think about a pink hippo, the more you will think about it. However, if you don't get emotionally charged by thoughts and just let them be, they will go as quickly as they came. Just like clouds in the sky, let them float by; granted, this takes practice, but with meditation and mindfulness, it can be done. It is important to work on your negative self-talk as it can be quite harmful.

Also notice where the negative thoughts are coming from. "The inner critic isn't harmless. It inhibits you, limits you, and stops you from pursing the life you truly want to live. It robs you of peace of mind and emotional well-being and, if left unchecked long enough, it can even lead to serious mental health problems such as depression or anxiety," says Dr. Jennice Vilhauer, director of Emory University's Adult Outpatient Psychotherapy Program in the Department of Psychiatry and Behavioral Science in the School of Medicine in Mayo Clinic. She states in the article, "the positive thinking that usually comes with optimism is a key part of effective stress management. And effective stress management is associated with many health benefits." The mindset strategies in Chapter Eleven provide much help on working with your thoughts and feelings to choose more positive ones.

Additionally, according to a 2014 peer-reviewed study by Veronika Engert, Jonathan Smallwood, and Tania Singer, "Research shows that negative cognitive styles are associated with increased stress reactivity, low mood, and accelerated cellular aging. . . . Our results indicate a fundamental link between the thoughts and stress levels we experience." So, you can literally think yourself into feeling younger, being calmer, and being more productive.

Here's a list of five activities that will help you essentially hack your stress and manage it in the moment:

- Box Breathing: To use this technique, Anna Gotter suggests on *Healthline.com* you breathe in to the count of four, hold your breath for a count of four, exhale slowly to the count of four, and keep air out of your lungs for a count of four. You can repeat this pattern as many times as you need.
- Be positive and let yourself feel what you need to feel, but don't sulk.
- Remember the law of attraction: you create your own reality. Where your focus goes, energy flows.
- Make a habit of using positive words. Don't say, "I wish I didn't feel anxious, or I feel anxious," because you are identifying with it and resisting your reality. Instead,

say, "Oh, okay, there's anxiety, no big deal." Another example is, instead of saying, "I hope I don't get sick," say, "I am healthy."

- Fake it until you make it; act the way you want to feel. If you want to be happy, then act happy. Your body language will change, which will change your thoughts, behaviors, and eventually your mood.

One more thing, as I have already shown in Chapter Eleven, it's important to have a growth mindset. Instead of saying, "I am not good at giving presentations," say, "I am not good at giving presentations *yet*." This shift in language will take you from a fixed place to a place of growth and improvement, and doing so begins with awareness of which mindset you're in and which one you want to be in.

THE EASY BUTTON

The "Easy Button" from Staples, an office supply store, made me wonder what the big deal was about this simple, kind of stupid, device. It is a big red button that says "Easy" on it. Then the brilliance of it occurred to me: When you complete a task and hit the Easy Button, the button says, "That was easy!" This sends a message to the brain reinforcing the idea that it *was* easy. It's a sort of cognitive-behavioral approach to processing information and changes our perception of the situation.

For instance, the task we completed may have been difficult, but if we press the easy button and repeat, "that was easy," then it may be stored by the brain as an easy task.

We will start believing it wasn't that hard after all, that we completed the task and, well, it was easy. It's also a great way to send a message to the brain that a task was completed, which helps with stress relief. Identifying a task as complete is a great way to gain some confidence and some relief. Staples even suggests the Easy Button be used as a stress relief device.

GRATITUDE AND FORGIVENESS

We have heard the advice to "practice gratitude" in many places, and I think at this point we may even dismiss it as a platitude. However, when you focus with your heart and mind while sitting in gratitude, you will feel your heart lighten. With social media always in our face, it is easy for us to look at others and say, "Wow, look at her, she's in Jamaica while I'm sitting at home in my sweats," and that thought devalues our present moment. Instead of seeing I have a roof over my head, I am healthy and living my best life in my sweats, I am now wanting to be somewhere else and be someone else. I am no longer grateful for what I have, rather I am looking at what I don't have. That's why my mom always told me to focus on my blessings and what I have, not what I don't have.

The same goes with work; you may compare yourself to others who may be excelling at work and feel less about yourself. Elizabeth Scott writes about a research study of highly stressed health care workers in a 2021 *Verywell Mind* article called "9 Simple Ways to Deal With Stress at Work." The goal was to improve the workers' outlooks using gratitude and forgiveness journals. The way it works is to jot down specific things you're grateful for. Instead of rushing to hurt or anger when someone behaves thoughtlessly toward you, choose forgiveness, and write about it. Interestingly, the study revealed after twelve weeks that the workers reported they were happier and more satisfied with their lives.

As you practice these skills, you may find your happiness level increasing too. Ready to focus on improving your happiness? There may be an even bigger payoff for you. Scott also cites research that shows when people focused more on kindness and other good works, they not only felt happier but also developed a stronger ability to fight off disease. Now that's a win-win.

ENDING THE DAY ON A STRONG NOTE

In my experience, early on in any new activity, it is more important to celebrate the days you do something positive and not worry about the days you don't. As you incorporate these new habits, take time at the end of each day—and really throughout the day—to take pride in these changes you're making for yourself. Celebrating your successes is very important because your body releases endorphins and you feel even happier. Celebrating feels great physically, and it also reinforces the wanted behavior. Bill Carmody points out, in "3 Reasons Celebrating Your Many Accomplishments Is Critical to Your Success" in *Inc.*, you can retrain your brain by celebrating. Celebrate the run, the good eating, the writing, the meditation, and don't fixate on the next time ... yet. With all this applause for yourself, you're much more likely to quiet your mind and sleep without worries or anxiety about the what ifs.

As I discussed in Chapter Three, sleep is an extremely important factor in your mental and physical health. Sleep is one of the most important factors to living a happier and less stressful life, and lack of sleep can be a trigger for anxiety. To get great sleep, take a few simple steps Rudy Mawer offers in "17 Proven Tips to Sleep Better at Night" in *Healthline*: avoid blue light (the light that can come from computer and smartphone screens), especially shortly before bedtime, and avoid caffeine in the afternoon. Keep your bedroom quiet. You'll also tend to get better sleep if you exercised earlier in the day (but exercise right before bed can disrupt your sleep).

You may also consider using a supplement like melatonin to help you get your forty winks. Consider melatonin as a last resort, since using it can upset your body's natural sleep cycles. If you struggle to fall asleep, use a weighted blanket (it feels like you are being hugged!), eye mask, essential oils such as lavender on your pillow, sleep meditations, and relaxing music. Weighted blankets have been shown to help with anxiety and stress as well as restless leg syndrome. According to R. Ackerly, Gaby Badre, and H. Olausson in their article for *Journal of Sleep Medicine & Disorders 2*, weighted blankets make it easier to fall asleep and improve sleep, leaving users feeling more refreshed in the morning. Amy Clapp notes in "Effects of Weighted Blankets on College Students' Anxiety" in digital commons at IWU that weighted blankets have also been shown to improve sleep quality and decrease anxiety for college students. What a simple thing to try that just might help you get more and more restful sleep.

CONCLUSION

Happiness may not be as far out of reach as you might have thought when you first picked up this book. When you manage your stress with consistent habits, over time you will choose how you feel over and over until it's second nature to think positively and make choices so you feel and work better. It all starts with a morning routine that leaves no room for stress and anxiety and continues throughout the day with activities to prevent stress and redirect it when it pops up. By the end of the day, you'll be looking at all the things you got right and set yourself up for a restful evening. It's time to be your most productive and happiest self—one habit at a time, so start somewhere and keep making progress.

CONCLUSION

My dear friends, I truly hope you found something in this book that resonated with you to help you lower your stress levels at work and in life. For the past four years, I put my whole heart and soul into this book in hopes that I could bring some serenity to your heart and to the world. I used to dream about the beautiful life I am living now, and there's no doubt you will get to where you want to be as well.

I know it's not always easy, and I know how much it can really suck, but trust me when I say that just like good times don't always last forever, neither do bad times. I hope this book encouraged you to see some of the light at the end of the tunnel. Learn to roll with the punches and accept the good with the bad. You can handle it, you've done it before, and you will do it again. In life, we will have our ups and downs, but learning to go with the flow makes it a little easier. Anxious thoughts and sensations can feel scary, but it is a liberating feeling when you finally stop fearing anxiety and befriend it instead.

When I was in the depths of my anxiety, I didn't know when good days would come again. After putting in the work, I finally saw results. You can read all you want, but if you don't take actionable steps, nothing will get done. So, don't fly toward your dreams, soar!

I know I dumped a lot of information and tips on you, and it may feel overwhelming. Like I mentioned before, take what serves you, and take it one habit at a time, one day at a time. If that feels like too much, then take it one hour at a time. Keep this book on your shelf, or in your desk, and come back to it when you need it. It'll always be there. You are not alone.

You can improve your situation at work by communicating your needs and advocating for yourself. No one is better than you, and you are not better than anyone else. Stand your ground! Take responsibility for your own joy, for your own health and happiness. No one is coming to save you and fix your life. You have the power in your hands. Taking care of yourself is far more important than being productive and perfect.

Stay in touch with me and be the first to know about my articles, speaking, services, and events at: www.massomaalam.com

Remember your physical and mental health is and should always come first and foremost. So, take that vacation, enjoy time with your family, and take care of yourself. You deserve to rest. I am rooting for you!

Oh, and lastly, don't forget to take your lunch break. *Wink.*

ACKNOWLEDGMENTS

First of all, I want to thank God, for giving me a second chance at life. Without God's grace, none of this would have been possible.

Thank you to my benevolent parents, Hyder and Unsar, and my siblings, Monis, Mohammad, and Fathima, for encouraging me to follow my dreams and finish this book.

Thank you to my husband, Omar, for being my rock. Thank you for loving me and holding my hand amidst my severe anxiety. Your love and acceptance healed me in more ways than you'll ever know.

Thank you to my kids, Rayaan and Amira, who gave me strength when I was weak. They say creation creates, so thank you for giving me inspiration and creativity to finish this book.

My sincere appreciation goes out to my editor, Cindy, whose diligent skills helped this book get to the next level.

Thank you to all my beta readers, especially Isaac and Summiaya, who gave this book the extra *oomph* it needed.

Thank you to all my interviewees for taking time out of their busy schedules to give my book life. Your insights and stories were so valuable in this book.

Lastly, thank you so much to my publisher New Degree Press and the entire team, especially Eric Koester, Brian Bies, and Sarah Lobrot, for being patient with me while I kept extending my deadlines. Without you, this book would not have been possible.

I would love to thank everyone who preordered my book and believed in its message. Special thanks to Thomas LoStracco for your generous contribution and for supporting my cause. I am also especially thankful to Omar Chohan, Hyder Alam, Unsar Tahira, Mohammad Alam, Monis Alam, Corey Burr, Thomas Folan, Chris Nicholas, John McGrath, Demetrios Agriantonis, Kevin T. Lie, Taniya Mohan, Mary Siragusa, Krystin Dauphin, Moiz Tayebaly, Jillian Martin, Rena Jolly, Ishita Wadhwani, Adnan Siddiqui, and Sobia Mirza for their very kind contributions to the publication of my book.

Thank you to all my first supporters:

Noureen Chohan	Tarandeep Sandhu
Zahid Chohan	Mir Alam
Mariam Chohan	Laila Naqvi
Shama Chohan	Miriam Meier
Samreen Kaur	Suzane Brikassa

Daniel Håkansson
Kanwal Baluch
Kanika Goyal
Maryam Malik
Seemal Khan
Anne Khan
Sahista Vahora
Anam Mir
Zoya Malik
Nazish Ahmed
Asma Ali
Khalid Memon
Sunia Tahir
Alyse Faour
Robert Schofield
Krystle Garcia
Mavara Agha
Faryal Siddiqui
Tehniyet Azam
Ariba Bhuvad
Nazia Khan
Seemab Navid
Arman Hamamah
Sherean Ali
Michael O'Hara
Hana Subedar
Ayesha Kiani
Tahmina Ahmed
Celeste Lai
Ahmad Rehmani
Simran Kaur
Jabran Mehta

Rima Khan
Bhavik Patel
Nimmy Martinus
Naureen Choudhary
Mia Mian
Angel Moreno
Neda Joby
Francisco Prada
Naaima Mufti
Aiman Masood
Sadaf Chaudhry
David Stern
Amnah Munir
Lori Burr
Fatima Zulqarnain
Adam Rind
Hunia Saghir
Amber Idris
Zehra Aftab
Sana Sheikh
Saima Qazi
Melissa Benbow
Audrey Nwokocha
Barbara Mulderig
Sarah Kham
Stacy Wystup
Subhajit Saha
Rehan Mustafa
Azka Afzal
Salman Malik
Bilal Khan
Samira Ateeq

Sukhjinder Chawla
Aysha Chengazi
Fatima Khan
Guneet Singh
Vaishaali Datta
Jessica Patel
Neelum Rana
Ria Ullal
Sindho Channa
Marilia Scalia
Danielle Croker
Sana Khan
Benazir Kaiser
Shaveta Malik
Mary Maybell
Nusrath Hussain
Kirti Patel
Amisha patel
Saara Arshad
Saadia Aslam
Ali Ahmad
Mahvish Ahmed
Isha Bhatti
Christopher Grilli
Sabina Mirza
Tariq Qasas
Benazeer Chaudhry
Nadiaa Ansari
Aneel Ursani
Zena Mufid
Suma Shah
Kiranprit Kaur

Reha Khan
Nancy Hussain
Shobha Kansal
Shiva Subance
Zeba Rashid
Mahwish shah
Hera Hyder
Amal Baig
Zainab Ahmed
Jillian Lehner
Sheena Kumra
Maya Wertheim
Sadaf Alam
Hassan Shahid
Neelam Bhagrath
Megan Heishman
Sonya Abed Ridha
Akhtar Qureshi
Christina Liu
Nimra Thanvi
Eric Koester
Zahra Ahsan
Stephanie Yang
Rahid Ali-Ludhianvi
Farah Mamji
Najia Khawar
Uzma Khayyam
Zofi Shaikh
Areeg Rehman
Carl Bolterstein
Amber Khan Mahmood
Faizah Khan

Emma Williams
Kelly Portillo
Huda Shaikh
Neelam Khan
Saira Khan
Ali Abidi
Robert Lundgren
Karan Mohan
Arooj Zia
Laura Wendling
Rabia Yousaf
Reema Cheema
Hira Kissana
Sofia Naseem
Waseem Stark
Amanda Jean Carucci
Sarah Syed
Zeshma Durrani
Raheela Syed
Rema Malik
Noor Khan
Deyanah othman
Zach Burr
Minahil imran
Safa Qazi
Amberin Shaikh
Usman Moghal
Taylor Jergens
Fahad Azam
Erin Grinstead
Natasha Shaikh
Michelle Audi

Abeera Shahid
Sumera Hussain
Darshika Patel
Aruna Radhakrishnan
Sai Radhakrishnan
Shahrukh Chaudhry
Mustafa Rehmani
Samir Khan
Maija Hall
Maha Chaudhry
Mahvish Banerjee
Kimberly Cohen
Anna Hertlein
Eda Ozturk
Alia Rind
Ali Ozenir
Chandan Samra
Calvin D'Souza
Aamna Mir
Shveta Alreja
Aisha Jamal
Tabish Khan
Zishan K.
Mubashar Khan
Faisal Kamal
Saba Ali
Amal Shariff
Hibah Aijaz
Sayeda Abbas
Anisha Bagga
Saher Aslam
Mariam Cheema

Haya Naseer
Neha Nandu
Hera Arham
Mariana Lockwood
Saira Ahmed
Asra Gilani
Mishi Ali
Mishqua Tate
Naureen Shahnawaz
Yasmeen Hafeez
Megan McKillip Wells
Aroosa Batool
Kiran Masood
Nitya Chandra
Farah Ahmed
Tamera Akarah
Aysha Chengazi
Tara Cotton
Kulsoom Sheriff
Mahnaz Sarfraz
Shirmeen Khan
Sadia Islam
Taj Khan
Mujtaba Alam
Aliza Khan
Umer Usman
Shaarmeen Chughtai
Kinza Hasan
Iqra Sheikh
Tulika Sahai
Amanie Akarah
Aziza Ejaz

Wahiba Bhuvad
Noorfatima Mahmood
Sophia Visanji
Sissey Kurian
Bisma Khan
Shabrin Haque
Samreen Arshad
Neenu Bains
Tabbster
Danya Sallaj
Nida Haque
Shifa Kanjwal
Tarannum khan
Manraj Khosla
Nazish Shah
Kim Lopez
Gurjoat Gill
Zohra Khan
Saira Zafar
Eiman Ashraf
Ajay Matta
Neel Talwar
Uneeb Khan
Sunita Gupta
Safia Massoud
Christina Prejean
Shah Alam Baloch
Aleeza Asghar
Resham Uttamchandani
Rabiya Samad
Hera Rehman
Richa Sahai

Jyotsna Magani
Dina Murshed
Yatzka Hernandez
Christiana Light
Sarah Ahmad
Angela Pucciarelli
Sarah Ansari
Urooj Karim

Mina Shahbaz
Nabeela Patail
Rachael Pelletter
Romi Kumari
Asfa Shad
Shahid Munir
Shaza Rizvi

APPENDIX

CHAPTER 1

Amador, Celia de San José. "Future of Work: 'No One Knows What the New Normal Is." *Allwork* (blog). August 14, 2020. https://allwork.space/2020/08/future-of-work-no-one-knows-what-the-new-normal-is/.

Anxiety and Depression Association of America. "Facts & Statistics." 2021. https://adaa.org/understanding-anxiety/facts-statistics

Arruda, William. "6 Ways COVID-19 Will Change The Workplace Forever." *Forbes*. May 7, 2020. https://www.forbes.com/sites/williamarruda/2020/05/07/6-ways-covid-19-will-change-the-workplace-forever/.

Barrero, Jose Maria, Nicholas Bloom, and Steven J. Davis. "Why Working From Home Will Stick." *Stanford.edu*. December 10, 2020. https://nbloom.people.stanford.edu/sites/g/files/sbiybj4746/f/why_wfh_stick1_0.pdf

Cassella, Megan. "The Pandemic Drove Women Out of the Workforce: Will They Come Back?" *Politico.com.* July 22, 2021. https://www.politico.com/news/2021/07/22/corona-virus-pandemic-women-workforce-500329

Franck, Thomas, and Nate Rattner. "Black and Hispanic Women Aren't Wining in the Job Market Recovery." *CNBC.com.* March 5, 2021. https://www.cnbc.com/2021/03/05/black-and-hispanic-women-arent-sharing-in-the-job-market-re-covery.html

Galloway, Steve. *Post Corona: From Crisis to Opportunity.* New York: Portfolio, 2020.

Gavidia, Matthew. "How Has COVID-19 Affected Mental Health, Severity of Stress Among Employees?" *American Journal of Managed Care.* April 20, 2020. https://www.ajmc.com/view/how-has-covid19-affected-mental-health-severity-of-stress-among-employees

The Government of Canada. "OSH Answers Fact Sheets: Work-place Stress—General." Canadian Centre for Occupational Health and Safety. 2018. https://www.ccohs.ca/oshanswers/psychosocial/stress.html.

Kamphaus, Randy, and Cecil R Reynolds. *Generalized Anxiety Disorder.* 300.02 (F41.1) Reprinted from American Psychiat-ric Association. *Diagnostic and Statistical Manual of Mental Disorders.* 5th ed. New York: American Psychiatric Publish-ing, 2013.

May, Katherine. *Wintering: The Power of Rest and Retreat in Difficult Times*. New York: Riverhead Books, 2020.

Panchal, Nirmita, et al. "The Implications of COVID-19 for Mental Health and Substance Use." *KFF.org*. August 21, 2020. https://www.kff.org/coronavirus-covid-19/issue-brief/the-implications-of-covid-19-for-mental-health-and-substance-use/.

Scott, Elizabeth. "Why Eustress Can Be Your Friend." *Verywell Mind*. 2020. https://www.verywellmind.com/what-you-need-to-know-about-eustress-3145109.

CHAPTER 2

Corinthian Colleges, Inc. "Workplace Stress on the Rise With 83% of Americans Frazzled by Something at Work." *Globe Newswire*. April 9, 2013. http://www.globenewswire.com/news-release/2013/04/09/536945/10027728/en/Workplace-Stress-on-the-Rise-With-83-of-Americans-Frazzled-by-Something-at-Work.html.

Dingman, Marc. "Know Your Brain: Amygdala." *Neuroscientifically Challenged* (blog). June 24, 2014. https://www.neuroscientificallychallenged.com/blog/know-your-brain-amygdala.

The Government of Canada. "OSH Answers Fact Sheets: Workplace Stress—General." Canadian Centre for Occupational Health and Safety. 2018. https://www.ccohs.ca/oshanswers/psychosocial/stress.html.

Goyal, Raj K., and Ikuo Hirano. "The Enteric Nervous System."
New England Journal of Medicine 334, no. 17 (1996): 1106–15.
https://doi.org/10.1056/NEJM199604253341707.

Kwik, Jim. "Performance Hacks with Dave Asprey." *Kwik Brain*
(blog). April 11, 2017. https://jimkwik.com/kwik-brain-009/.

Lipman, Victor. "Workplace Trend: Stress Is On The Rise." *Forbes*.
January 9, 2019. https://www.forbes.com/sites/victorlip-
man/2019/01/09/workplace-trend-stress-is-on-the-rise/.

Martin, Elizabeth I., et al. "The Neurobiology of Anxiety Disorders: Brain Imaging, Genetics, and Psychoneuroendocrinol-
ogy." *Psychiatric Clinics of North America* 32, no. 3 (September
2009): 549–75. https://doi.org/10.1016/j.psc.2009.05.004.

Northwestern Medicine. "The Science of Anxiety (Infographic)."
2021. https://www.nm.org/healthbeat/healthy-tips/emo-
tional-health/the-science-of-anxiety.

CHAPTER 3

Albert, Michelle A., Donna K. Arnett, Roger S. Blumenthal, et
al. "2019 ACC/AHA Guideline on the Primary Prevention of
Cardiovascular Disease: A Report of the American College
of Cardiology/American Heart Association Task Force on
Clinical Practice Guidelines." *Circulation*. American Heart
Association. (2019)140:11. https://www.ahajournals.org/
doi/10.1161/CIR.0000000000000678

American Psychological Association. "More Sleep Would Make
Most Americans Happier, Healthier and Safer." *APA.org*.

2004. http://www.apa.org/research/action/sleep-deprivation.aspx.

Bin Zarah, Aljazi, Juliana Enriquez-Marulanda, and Jeanette M. Andrade. "Relationship between Dietary Habits, Food Attitudes and Food Security Status among Adults Living within the United States Three Months Post-Mandated Quarantine: A Cross-Sectional Study." *Nutrients* 12, no. 11 (2020): 3468. https://doi.org/10.3390/nu12113468

Daley, Amanda. "Exercise and Depression: A Review of Reviews." *Journal of Clinical Psychology in Medical Settings* 15, no. 2 (June 2008): 140–47. https://doi.org/10.1007/s10880-008-9105-z.

Gonzalez, Michael J., and Jorge R. Miranda-Massari. "Diet and Stress." *Psychiatric Clinics of North America* 37, no. 4 (December 2014): 579–89. https://doi.org/10.1016/j.psc.2014.08.004.

Irwin, Michael, et al. "Partial Night Sleep Deprivation Reduces Natural Killer and Cellular Immune Responses in Humans." *The FASEB Journal* 10, no. 5 (April 1996): 643–53. https://doi.org/10.1096/fasebj.10.5.8621064.

Kujala, U. M. "Evidence on the Effects of Exercise Therapy in the Treatment of Chronic Disease." *British Journal of Sports Medicine* 43, no. 8 (August 1, 2009): 550–55. https://doi.org/10.1136/bjsm.2009.059808.

Mayo Clinic. "Exercise and Stress: Get Moving to Manage Stress." *Mayo Clinic Healthy Lifestyle*. August 18, 2020. https://www.mayoclinic.org/healthy-lifestyle/stress-management/in-depth/exercise-and-stress/art-20044469.

Odyssey. "About Us." *theodysseyonline.com.* July 1, 2019. https://
www.theodysseyonline.com/st/about.

Otto, Michael W., and Jasper A. J Smits. *Exercise for Mood and
Anxiety: Proven Strategies for Overcoming Depression and
Enhancing Well-Being.* New York: Oxford University Press,
2011.

Rogers, P.J. et al. "Caffeine and Anxiety." *Appetite* 47, no. 2 (September 2006): 274. https://doi.org/10.1016/j.appet.2006.07.057.

St. John, Bonnie, and Allen P. Haines. *Micro-Resilience: Minor
Shifts for Major Boosts in Focus, Drive, and Energy.* New York:
Center Street, 2017.

CHAPTER 4

Ardito, Rita B., and Daniela Rabellino. "Therapeutic Alliance
and Outcome of Psychotherapy: Historical Excursus, Mea-
surements, and Prospects for Research." *Frontiers in Psychology* 2 (2011). https://doi.org/10.3389/fpsyg.2011.00270.

Butler, A., et al. "The Empirical Status of Cognitive-Behavioral Therapy: A Review of Meta-Analyses." *Clinical Psychology Review* 26, no. 1 (January 2006): 17–31. https://doi.
org/10.1016/j.cpr.2005.07.003, p. 17.

CHAPTER 5

Ahmed, Idil, (@idillionaire). "You can rise up from anything.
You can completely recreate yourself. Nothing is permanent. You're not stuck. You have choices. You can think new

thoughts. You can learn something new. You can create new habits. All that matters is that you decide today and never look back." *Twitter.* August 7, 2018. https://twitter.com/idillionaire/status/1026982611632062464?lang=en.

Charney, Dennis S., and Steven M. Southwick. *Resilience: The Science of Mastering Life's Greatest Challenges.* New York: Cambridge University Press, 2012.

Loehr Jim, and Tony Schwartz. *The Power of Full Engagement.* New York: Simon and Schuster, 2003.

St. John, Bonnie, and Allen P. Haines. *Micro-Resilience: Minor Shifts for Major Boosts in Focus, Drive, and Energy.* New York: Center Street, 2017.

CHAPTER 6

Lupu, Ioana, and Mayra Ruiz-Castro. "Work-Life Balance Is a Cycle, Not an Achievement." *Harvard Business Review.* January 29, 2021. https://hbr.org/2021/01/work-life-balance-is-a-cycle-not-an-achievement.

Ziegler, Sheryl. "How to Let Go of Working-Mom Guilt." *Harvard Business Review.* September 4, 2020. https://hbr.org/2020/09/how-to-let-go-of-working-mom-guilt.

CHAPTER 7

Cameron, Laurie. *The Mindful Day: Practical Ways to Find Focus, Calm and Joy from Morning to Evening.* Washington: National Geographic, 2018.

Kondo, Marie, and Scott Sonenshein. *Joy at Work: Organizing Your Professional Life*. New York: Little Brown & Company, 2020.

Melton, Jake. *Minimize to Maximize Your Happiness: Cut the Crap.* McKinney: J.B. Melton Group, 2018.

OfficeMax. "An Unorganized Nation: Americans Seek Ways to Improve Organizational Skills to Maintain Peace of Mind Even Though Many Are Critical of Themselves and Their Messy Colleagues." *PR NewsWire.* January 2011. http://multivu.prnewswire.com/mnr/officemax/46659/docs/46659-NewsWorthy_Analysis.pdf.

St. John, Bonnie, and Allen P. Haines. *Micro-Resilience: Minor Shifts for Major Boosts in Focus, Drive, and Energy.* New York: Center Street, 2017.

CHAPTER 8

Alam, Massoma. "Go Spaghetti: Overcoming Anxiety." *YouTube.com.* TEDx Wilmington Live. June 14, 2018. https://www.youtube.com/watch?v=HAEIMLnCSAk

DARE Response. *DareResponse.com.* 2021. https://www.dare-response.com/

Kinney, Jane. "Productivity and Procrastination: How to Maximize Your Efficiency." *Zenerations.* January 11, 2021. https://zenerations.org/2021/01/11/productivity-and-procrastination-how-to-maximize-your-efficiency/.

Lieberman, Charlotte. "Why You Procrastinate (It Has Nothing to Do With Self-Control)." *The New York Times*, March 25, 2019. https://www.nytimes.com/2019/03/25/smarter-living/why-you-procrastinate-it-has-nothing-to-do-with-self-control.html.

McDonagh, Barry. *Dare: The New Way to End Anxiety and Stop Panic Attacks*. United States: Dare People Pty, Limited, 2015.

"The Zeigarnik Effect Explained." *Psychologist World*. Memory Psychology. 2021.

https://www.psychologistworld.com/memory/zeigarnik-effect-interruptions-memory

CHAPTER 9

Brees, Jeremy, Mark Martinko, and Paul Harvey. "Abusive Supervision: Subordinate Personality or Supervisor Behavior?" *Journal of Managerial Psychology* 31, no. 2 (March 14, 2016). https://doi.org/10.1108/JMP-04-2014-0129.

Cuncic, Arlin. "How to Practice Active Listening." *Verywell Mind*. May 25, 2020. https://www.verywellmind.com/what-is-active-listening-3024343.

Desmarais, Serge, Kevin E. Kelloway, and A.C.H. Schat. "Prevalence of Workplace Aggression in the U.S. Workforce: Findings from a National Study." *Handbook of Workplace Violence* (Thousand Oaks: Sage, 2006), 47–89. Quoted in Tepper, Bennett J. "Abusive Supervision in Work Organizations: Review, Synthesis, and Research Agenda." *Journal* of *Management* 33, no. 3 (June 2007): 261–89. https://doi. org/10.1177/0149206307300812.

Heathfield, Susan. "How to Deal With a Bully at Work." *The Balance Careers*. May 31, 2020. https://www.thebalanceca-reers.com/how-to-deal-with-a-bully-at-work-1917901.

Korn Ferry. "Workplace Stress Continues to Mount." *KornFerry. com* n.d. https://www.kornferry.com/insights/articles/workplace-stress-motivation.

Lowry, Ann, and Amy Overton. "Conflict Management: Difficult Conversations with Difficult People." *Clinics in Colon and Rectal Surgery* 26, no. 04 (November 20, 2013): 259–64. https://doi.org/10.1055/s-0033-1356728.

Taibbi, Robert. "The Art of Solving Relationship Problems." *Psychology Today*. January 17, 2011. https://www.psycholo-gytoday.com/us/blog/fixing-families/201101/the-art-solv-ing-relationship-problems.

Tepper, Bennett J. et al. "Procedural Injustice, Victim Preparation, and Abusive Supervision." *Personnel Psychology* 59 (2006). p. 119.

Ziv, Stav. "Don't Let Workplace Bullies Win—Here's How to Spot Them and Stop Them." *Themuse* (blog). n.d. https://www.themuse.com/advice/how-to-deal-with-workplace-bullies.

CHAPTER 10

Agrawal, Sangeeta, and Ben Wigert. "Employee Burnout, Part 1: The 5 Main Causes." *Gallup Workplace* (blog). July 12, 2018. https://www.gallup.com/workplace/237059/employee-burnout-part-main-causes.aspx.

Cooper, Belle Beth. "8 Reasons Why You Should Definitely Take That Lunch Break." *Fast Company*. March 12, 2014. https://www.fastcompany.com/3027496/8-reasons-why-you-should-definitely-take-that-lunch-break.

Goulet, Emily. "Adam Grant Is (Not) Superman." *Philadelphia*. October 27, 2018. https://www.phillymag.com/business/2018/10/27/adam-grant-wharton-books-business/.

Grant, Adam. *Give and Take: A Revolutionary Approach to Success*. New York: Viking, 2013.

"How to Prevent Employee Burnout." *Gallup Workplace* (blog), 2021. https://www.gallup.com/workplace/313160/preventing-and-dealing-with-employee-burnout.aspx

Leonard, Thomas. "Teams with Role Clarity Are Substantially More Successful than Teams Without." *Organizational Diagnostics & Development Oddblog*. n.d. http://www.theoddcompany.ie/oddblog/teams-with-role-clarity-are-substantially-more-successful-than-teams-without/.

Middleton, Jackie. "7 Health Benefits of Taking Your Lunch Break." *Best Health*. July 16, 2019. https://www.besthealthmag.ca/best-you/health/benefits-of-lunch-breaks/.

National Public Radio. "We're Not Taking Enough Lunch Breaks. Why That's Bad For Business." Here and Now. *NPR.* March 5, 2015. https://www.npr.org/sections/the-salt/2015/03/05/390726886/were-not-taking-enough-lunch-breaks-why-thats-bad-for-business.

Patel, Gayatri. "Role Clarity Is Important to Establish an Effective Team." *LinkedIn* (blog). May 11, 2016. https://www.linkedin.com/pulse/role-clarity-important-establish-effective-team-gayatri-patel/.

World Health Organization. "Burn-out an 'Occupational Phenomenon': International Classification of Diseases." *World Health Organization International.* News. May 28, 2019. https://www.who.int/news/item/28-05-2019-burn-out-an-occupational-phenomenon-international-classification-of-diseases.

CHAPTER 11

Dweck, Carol. *Mindset: The New Psychology of Success.* Updated ed. New York: Ballantine, 2011.

Manson, Mark. *The Subtle Art of Not Giving a Fuck: A Counterintuitive Approach to Living a Good Life.* New York: HarperOne, 2016.

Pillay, Srini. "Anticipatory Anxiety: The Suffering and Solutions." *Psychology Today* (blog). January 26, 2011. https://www.psychologytoday.com/us/blog/debunking-myths-the-mind/201101/anticipatory-anxiety-the-suffering-and-solutions.

Popova, Maria. "Fixed vs. Growth: The Two Basic Mindsets That Shape Our Lives." *Brainpickings.com*. January 29, 2014. https://www.brainpickings.org/2014/01/29/carol-dweck-mindset/.

CHAPTER 12

Ackerly, R., Gaby Badre, and H Olausson. "Positive Effects of a Weighted Blanket on Insomnia." *Journal of Sleep Medicine & Disorders* 2, no. 3 (2015).

Burke, Claire. "Distracted in the office? Blame evolution." *The Guardian*. Future of Work. Guardian Careers. March 1, 2016. https://www.theguardian.com/careers/2016/mar/01/distracted-office-blame-evolution-workspace-design-focus

Cameron, Laurie. *The Mindful Day: Practical Ways to Find Focus, Calm and Joy from Morning to Evening.* Washington: National Geographic, 2018.

Carmody, Bill. "3 Reasons Celebrating Your Many Accomplishments Is Critical to Your Success." *Inc.* August 12, 2015. https://www.inc.com/bill-carmody/3-reasons-celebrating-your-many-accomplishments-is-critical-to-your-success.html.

Cascio, Christopher N., et al. "Self-Affirmation Activates Brain Systems Associated with Self-Related Processing and Reward and Is Reinforced by Future Orientation." *Social Cognitive and Affective Neuroscience* 11, no. 4 (April 1, 2016): 621–29. https://doi.org/10.1093/scan/nsv136.

Clapp, Amy. "Effects of Weighted Blankets on College Students' Anxiety." Digital Commons at IWU. *Illinois Wesleyan University.com.* 2019. https://digitalcommons.iwu.edu/nursing_honproj/51.

Covey, Stephen R. *The 7 Habits of Highly Effective People: Restoring the Character Ethic.* Rev. ed. New York: Free Press, 2004.

Debrot, Anik, et al. "Daily Work Stress and Relationship Satisfaction: Detachment Affects Romantic Couples' Interactions Quality." *Journal of Happiness Studies* 19, no. 8 (December 2018): 2283–2301. https://doi.org/10.1007/s10902-017-9922-6.

Engert, Veronika, Jonathan Smallwood, and Tania Singer. "Mind Your Thoughts: Associations between Self-Generated Thoughts and Stress-Induced and Baseline Levels of Cortisol and Alpha-Amylase." *Biological Psychology* 103 (December 2014): 283–91. https://doi.org/10.1016/j.biopsycho.2014.10.004.

Gardner, Benjamin, Phillippa Lally, and Jane Wardle. "Making Health Habitual: The Psychology of 'Habit-Formation' and General Practice." *British Journal of General Practice* 62, no. 605 (December 2012): 664–66. https://doi.org/10.3399/bjgp12X659466.

Gotter, Ann. "Box Breathing," *Healthline.* June 17, 2020. https://www.healthline.com/health/box-breathing.

Innerfire BV. "Cold Therapy." *Wim Hof Method.com,* 2021. https://www.wimhofmethod.com/cold-therapy

King, Stephen. *On Writing: A Memoir of the Craft.* New York: Scribner, 2000.

Kwik, Jim. *Limitless: Upgrade Your Brain, Learn Anything Faster, and Unlock Your Exceptional Life.* 1st edition. Carlsbad: Hay House, 2020.

Lally, Philippa, Cornelia H.M. van Jaarsveld, Henry.W.W. Potts, and Jane Wardle. "How are habits formed: Modelling habit formation in the real world." *European Journal of Social Psychology.* (July 16, 2009): 40: 998-1009. https://doi.org/10.1002/ejsp.674

Lambert, Kelly. *Lifting Depression: A Neuroscientist's Hands-on Approach to Activating Your Brain's Healing Power.* New York: Basic Books, 2010.

Luscombe, Belinda. "Do We Need $75,000 a Year to Be Happy?" *TIME.* September 6, 2010. http://content.time.com/time/magazine/article/0,9171,2019628,00.html.

Marksberry, Kellie. "Top 5 Workplace Stress Busting Tips." *The American Institute of Stress.* July 18, 2012. https://www.stress.org/top-5-workplace-stress-busting-tips.

Mawer, Rudy. "17 Proven Tips to Sleep Better at Night." *Healthline.* February 28, 2020. https://www.healthline.com/nutrition/17-tips-to-sleep-better.

Michels, David. "Staples Easy Button gets IoT makeover." *Talking Points.* August 28, 2017. https://talkingpointz.com/staples-easy-button-gets-iot-makeover/

Scott, Elizabeth. "9 Simple Ways to Deal With Stress at Work." *VeryWellMind.com.* July 31, 2021.

https://www.verywellmind.com/how-to-deal-with-stress-at-work-3145273

Smith, Scott. "Breaking Habits Now or Later." *Daily Boost.* Apple Podcast. August 9, 2021. https://podcasts.apple.com/us/podcast/daily-boost-daily-coaching-and-motivation/

Stevenson, Jason. @Jason Stevensen—Sleep Meditation Music. "Affirmations for Health, Wealth, and Abundance "I Am." *YouTube.com.* December 10, 2017. https://www.youtube.com/watch?v=GnWlERKoUJc

UshersNewLook. "5 Rules to Follow as You Find Your Spark." *YouTube.com.* Video, 16:50. October 17, 2016. https://youtu.be/8l-YpiiBH4o.

Vilhauer, Jennice. "4 Ways to Stop Beating Yourself Up, Once and For All." Psychology Today. March 18, 2016. https://www.psychologytoday.com/us/blog/living-forward/201603/4-ways-stop-beating-yourself-once-and-all.

Made in United States
Orlando, FL
28 January 2023

29153709R00130